THE SILVER NEW NOTHING

ALSO BY SYBIL MARSHALL

Everyman's Book of English Folk Tales
Fenland Chronicle
Once Upon A Village

THE SILVER NEW NOTHING

EDWARDIAN CHILDHOOD IN THE FEN

SYBIL MARSHALL

Illustrated by Ewart Oakeshott

THE BOYDELL PRESS

© Sybil Marshall 1987

First published 1987 by The Boydell Press
an imprint of Boydell & Brewer Ltd
PO Box 9, Woodbridge, Suffolk IP12 3DF
and Wolfeboro, N.H. 03894–2069

ISBN 0 85115 461 1

British Library Cataloguing in Publication Data
Marshall, Sybil
The silver new nothing : Edwardian
childhood in the Fen.
1. Fens (England)—Social life and
customs
I. Title
942.6'54082'0922   DA670.F33

Photoset and printed in Great Britain by
Redwood Burn Limited, Trowbridge, Wiltshire

CONTENTS

for Lois
and the memory of Gerald
with love

AUTHOR'S FOREWORD

'Is it true?'

The answer to that question, posed at the end of any story, is usually an equivocal one. It depends what you mean by Truth. The scraps of silk in my patchwork quilt are nonetheless silk for my having re-arranged them into a new whole.

This book is made up of scraps from the past. It is not an autobiography, because it comes to an end when I was five. It cannot be graced with the title of memoirs, because most of the incidents do not concern me. I know about them only because I heard them related over and over again, and lived among the people they concerned.

Though the period and the locality are fixed firmly in reality, that does not make this book a documentary. There are few records to prove or disprove anything I have written. In any case, the people these tales are about were of no importance to anybody but each other. All the same, they were once as much flesh and blood as King Solomon or The Queen of Sheba, and are now, like those royal personages, 'gone – all gone'. Of all those characters who live again for a brief hour or two in these pages, only one other besides myself remains – my sister Lois*, whom in the book I have called Tod.

Why then, have I given her and my brother Gerald (along with a few others) fictional names? Or allowed Gerald, in the voice of the boy he once was, to tell my tales for me?

I don't know. It came like that from the end of my pen, and seemed right, somehow. Perhaps I was seeking truth uncon-

* Lois died while this book was in production.

vii

sciously, the truth of honesty to my readers that I couldn't vouch absolutely for all that I was writing.

This book is very nearly, though not exactly, a sequel to *Fenland Chronicle*, but it is not quite so factual, nor so convincingly at first-hand as the stories of my father and mother were.

In both the books, all the same, the main protagonists are all members of my own immediate family. That makes the books into true sagas, as in the old Norse sense. They are tales told of the doings of one's kinsmen, in order that memories of the people themselves and of their deeds and utterances shall not die with them. For that reason, in my own two books, the members of my family (apart from Lois and Gerald) have all been given their proper names, or, as in the case of Grandad Rattles (John Thomas Papworth), the name he was always known by. I can name them all thus because they are my kinsmen, and 'belong' to me.

Others – though mostly dear old friends and neighbours, do not 'belong' so exclusively to me. I have chosen deliberately to leave them cloaked in the dignity of anonymity, honoured by it in the same way as is *The Unknown Soldier* who lies buried in Westminster Abbey as a symbol by which one may stand for all.

The way they endured and accepted hardship, not with a stoic indifference, but in accord with their belief in a Providence who 'worked in a mysterious way His wonders to perform', and who therefore might prove stern or benevolent towards them, but from whose all-seeing eyes not one of them could hide: their ironic humour, so often turned only against themselves and their own shortcomings: their physical toughness, combined with an inner sensitivity for the more spiritual aspects of life: and their capacity for laughter and enjoyment whenever occasion and opportunity offered it to them. These are not just the characteristics of my own folk, but of all those old fenlanders in general – in my admittedly biassed view, the very salt of the earth. The portraits I paint of them are true reflections, just as their vernacular voices are true echoes of the past.

Every hexagon of silk in the patchwork quilt I have recently completed is a scrap that sometime, somewhere, existed before in a different form, and had a significance quite other than that it now has for me. My brother Gerald's necktie, for instance. His widow, giving it to me for my patchwork, said it was one he was so fond of that 'he nearly lived and died in it'. But when I, too, am gone, no one else will know exactly which motif in the quilt is made from that particular tie. It will simply have taken its place among all the others as part of a newly-created entity: but the truth that it was once my brother's favourite neck-tie still stands, unaltered and unalterable.

So with the scraps of memory that have gone into the making of this book. They have been trimmed and stitched together, not always exactly as they were in reality, but in such a way as to make plain a picture of the times, the place, and the community common to them all.

Let me give a specific example. One incident for which there is still plenty of documentary evidence is the flood in the disastrous summer of 1912, when corn stood up to the bands of the sheaves in water, and when what harvest was saved was fetched in by boat. It was then that my brother and his friend did in truth launch their tub, and got stuck out in the wastes of water. But the equally true incident when the friend's quick and courageous action saved my brother from drowning took place at a different time, when they were in mischief again together. I had heard nothing about the second incident until the rescuer died, in his late sixties. Then my brother, grieving for his old mate, told me, and said 'An' I reckon he died keeping his promise to me never to tell a soul what happened that day. It was my fault. We'd been warned, and told many a time not to go there.' Does it really matter that I have here stitched one happening to the other?

Some of the scraps were not big enough in themselves to

use without some imaginative additions, as in *Helping Dobson*. The spy my Aunt Harriet had as a lodger was a fact. His was not a tale, though, to be told with delight over the fireside in after years. The bare facts were all I ever heard, and even they were censored. I had to supply the details for myself, then as now.

Other remnants I found in my memory box were rejected for a different reason. I recently took from its drawer the huge blue-and-gold neckerchief of silk that once upon a time Dad used to wrap round his fiddle – the very same one that in *Helping Dobson* Jed borrowed in the hope of catching a live adder. I had intentions of cutting it up and putting it with Gerald's tie into my patchwork. But once it was in my hands again, the sight and feel of it, and most of all the faint, elusive scent of it, brought memories so powerful they were too strong for me. It stays where it is, 'a silver new nothing' too precious to be brought out and shared with anybody – as with some other poignant tales I could have included in this book, but chose not to.

One or two of the stories had to be reshaped, rather than added to. 'Old Oamy' was as real as I am, but the treasure in his little box was nothing more than a figment of his disordered imagination. Does it matter that from the many tales he told us I have chosen to turn his treasure into that silver new nothing that was dangled so tantalisingly before me during my earliest years?

My childhood is now almost as remote in time as its setting was then in place. I can view it only through a spy-glass of memory that is at least seven decades long, and as always when looking through a lens from the wrong end, the picture is vivid but a long way off. It may be that events have become telescoped occasionally, as well. Time plays curious tricks.

Truth, they say, lies at the bottom of a well. It is hardly ever retrieved whole and untarnished; but I have done my best.

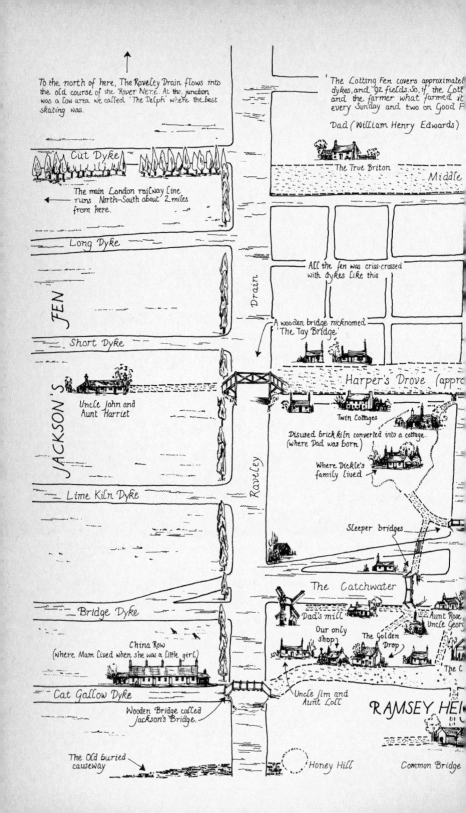

To the north of here, The Raveley Drain flows into the old course of the River Nene. At the junction was a low area we called 'The Delph' where the best skating was.

'The Lotting Fen covers approximatel[y] dykes, and 92 fields. So, if the Lott[ing] and the farmer what farmed it every Sunday and two on Good F[riday]

Dad (William Henry Edwards)

The True Briton

Middle

Cut Dyke

The main London railway line runs North-South about 2 miles from here.

Long Dyke

FEN

Drain

All the fen was criss-crossed with dykes like this

A wooden bridge nicknamed 'The Tay Bridge'

Short Dyke

Harper's Drove (appro[x]

JACKSON'S

Uncle John and Aunt Harriet

Twin Cottages

Disused brick kiln converted into a cottage. (where Dad was born)

Where Dickle's family lived

Lime Kiln Dyke

Raveley

Sleeper bridges

The Catchwater

Bridge Dyke

Dad's mill

Aunt Rose Uncle Geor[ge]

China Row (where Mam lived when she was a little girl)

Our only shop

The Golden Drop

The C[

Cat Gallow Dyke

Wooden Bridge called Jackson's Bridge.

Uncle Jim and Aunt Loll

RAMSEY HEI[

The Old buried causeway

Honey Hill

Common Bridge

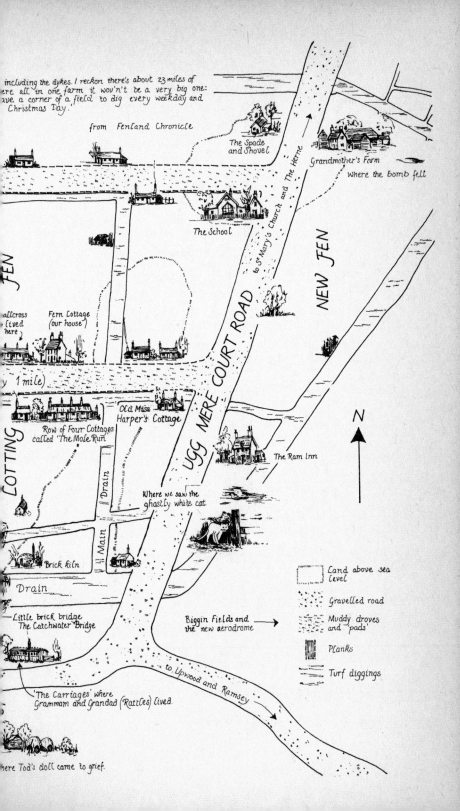

including the dykes. I reckon there's about 23 miles of [?]ere all in one farm it wou'n't be a very big one: [?]ave a corner of a field to dig every weekday and Christmas Day.

from Fenland Chronicle

The Spade and Shovel

Grandmother's Farm

where the Bomb fell

The School

to St Mary's Church and The Herne

NEW FEN

FEN

allcross (lived here)

Fern Cottage (our house)

UGG MERE COURT ROAD

(y 1 mile)

LOTTING

Row of Four Cottages called 'The Mole Run'

Old Miss Harper's Cottage

Drain

Main

The Ram Inn

Where we saw the ghastly white cat.

Brick kiln

Drain

Biggin Fields and the new aerodrome

Little brick bridge The Catchwater Bridge

N

Land above sea level

Gravelled road

Muddy droves and 'pads'

Planks

Turf diggings

to Upwood and Ramsey

'The Carriages' where Grammam and Grandad (Rattles) lived.

[?]here Tod's doll came to grief.

THE SILVER

NEW NOTHING

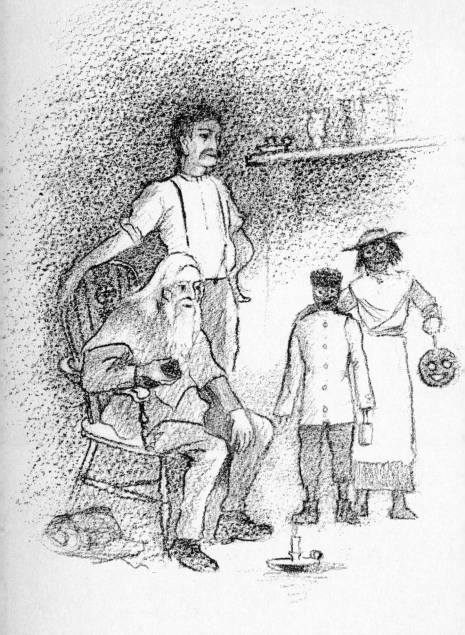

WE HAD JUST sat down to tea. It was still barely four o'clock, but Dad had lit the lamp already, and stood it down on the middle of the tea table. He had left off work early, to be in the house and finished his tea by the time we wanted to get ready. We had run all the way home from school, nearly a mile, and we were still hot from the exertion, though it had begun to snow a little, small, dry flakes in the bitter wind that was blowing across the fen.

'Too cold for snow,' Dad said, 'I reckon there won't be much till it gets a bit warmer. The wind's perishing cold, though. Goes right through you.'

We didn't want any tea, but we had too much sense to say so. It would be another hour and a half before we could dress ourselves up, and we knew Mam wouldn't let us set out without food inside us. All our friends from school would be sitting down to a cooked tea, because we were the only family for miles around that didn't have the main meal of the day when the horses were unyoked in the afternoon. So our play-mates would set off stuffed with salt pork and onion dumpling. We felt lucky that all we'd got to get down in our excitement was bread and jam.

There was still an hour and a half to go before they would let us get ready. We didn't know how we were going to get through the time.

Mam was filling the tea-pot from the kettle on the hob by the blazing fire on the hearth. She was turning back to the table when she happened to glance out of the window, where the dusk was by now over, and darkness falling early, because of the heavy clouds.

'There's somebody coming' she said to Dad. Dad looked

round, and was just in time to see a sacking-covered figure pass between two bushes before it disappeared again behind the thick hedge that ran along the house side of the path.

'Jimmy's brother Ted' said Dad, and gave his attention again to spreading beef dripping on his toast. The toast was hot, and as fast as he put the dripping on, it melted, till it ran through and made a pool on his plate. That was how he liked it, covered with a thick layer of salt.

Tod, my sister (her name was Lois, but nobody ever called her anything but Tod) and I scrambled down and ran to the window. We understood quite well from what Dad had said that what he had seen was a wandering tramp, because in our part of the country all tramps were called 'Jimmy's brother Ted'. I never did find out why.

'Is it Old Oamy?' we said. 'Dad is it Old Oamy?'

'Sit down and eat your tea' said Mam sharply. 'We shall know soon enough.' Then when we didn't obey her at once, she said 'Do you hear me, Jed? Come back to the table!' (I was christened Gerald, but everybody's always called me Jed.)

We went back to the table reluctantly and gobbled the bread and jam Mam had put on our plates.

If it was Old Oamy, we couldn't ask for more. As Tod said afterwards 'our cup runnethed over'. It didn't sound quite right, but I knew what she meant.

The time just after Christmas always dragged, when the presents were no longer new, and the visitors had gone home, and all the family parties were over for another year. The days were so short that Tod and me started up the drove to school before it was properly light, and had to run home if we wanted to get there before it was nearly dark again. When it snowed properly, it was exciting for a day or two, but we soon got fed up with being wet and cold in school all day after pelting each other with snowballs, and rolling about in it. Our feet got sodden in spite of our good boots and were lumps of ice for the rest of the day. Snow was a short-lived pleasure, though we didn't like to admit it. The only thing

4

that made the first week of the new year bearable at all was the thought of plough-witching night, on the second Monday of January.

But this year it had somehow been different. For one thing, our Grammam had come to stop with us for Christmas. She had been took bad, and had to go to bed. So she didn't go home, but stopped on where Mam could look after her. She'd soon got well enough to be able to get up and sit in Mam's rocking chair, and we loved to see her there. Tod would sit on the hearthrug with her new doll and the cat, as close to Grammam's knees as she could get, while I sat at the table with my paintbox or my lead soldiers. Then Grammam would sing, hymns and old songs, and when her voice gave out, she'd whistle. She could whistle so true you'd think it was a bird, only she whistled tunes that we knew, and the birds didn't.

Our Grandad never stopped at our house. He didn't come even to dinner on Christmas Day or Boxing Day, because he always went as a beater for Sir John's shoot on Boxing Day, and spent the day before getting ready for it, so he said. We all understood perfectly well what getting ready for it meant – stopping as long in the pub as he could with what money he'd got. But in any case he was nobody for family gatherings, being the black sheep of the whole village. Our Mam was ashamed of him, and was glad he didn't come, because then Grammam could come by herself and enjoy being without him. Sometimes Grandad would get into one of his rampages, as Dad called them, and not let her come either, but this year he hadn't made a fuss at all, even when she couldn't go home when Christmas was over. Instead, he'd called nearly every night to see her – at least, that's what he said and Grammam believed. Mam said it was to collect enough grub to last him through the next day, and Dad said that if Rattles wasn't his father-in-law, he'd lock the door of the hovel where he kept the pig food. Grandad kept pigs, of course, like everybody else, but somehow he never had to buy any pollard, or other food for them. Dad knew very well who fed

Rattles's pigs most of the time; but he was never a man to make a fuss, and as he said many a time to Mam, what would Grammam have to eat it they hadn't got a pig to kill now and then?

So there had been the added pleasure (for me, that is) of seeing Grandad Rattles nearly every evening. He liked me, and I liked him, but he seemed to hate Tod, and never spoke to her if he could help it. He was always looking for things to bring me when he went for jaunts across the fen, like birds' nests and eggs, and once, when I was about twelve, he brought an old rusty sword blade he'd found in Whittlesey Mere. And another time just before the plough-witching night I'm telling you about if I ever get to it, he'd brought a twisted root that looked for all the world like a wizened old man. When Dad saw it, he said 'That's a mandrake, ain't it?' and Rattles had replied 'Ah! I'm bin a-looking for one for many a year. Be careful how you 'andle it, Jed. If you handle him rough 'e'll let out such a screech as'll make the whull fen frit to goo to bed.'

When Mam saw it, she said she wouldn't have it in the house, the unlucky, evil old thing. So Dad had to take it away and hide it. Mam and Grammam were very set about things being unlucky, and took a lot of notice of o'ems, as they called them. (Dad told me the proper word was 'omens', and that they were all old wives' tales; but a robin in the house or an owl sitting on the roof would make even Dad uneasy, as we could see. So Tod and me reckoned he believed in the o'ems a bit in spite of himself, and that made us put real faith in them. As Tod said, we never had any lucky o'ems, and if the bad ones didn't come true you were so glad that you forgot about them anyway.)

Mam said the mandrake was bound to bring us bad luck, and that if it shrieked out we should hear it wherever Dad had put it. Then it would mean a death before the year was out. One night the wind got up, and Tod woke up to hear it moaning down the drainpipes. She sat up in bed and screamed so loud that Dad ran into our bedroom in nothing but his shirt, to see what was the matter. Tod was staring at the wall with her great brown eyes wide open, like an owl's, and screaming 'it's the mandrake shrieking'. Dad calmed her down and told her it was only the wind in the drainpipe, so she went back to sleep. But in the morning, when they were talking about it, Grammam said under her breath to Mam (thinking we shouldn't hear) 'Ah, I heard it an' all. That's a good sign o' death as any mandrake. Mark my words, there'll be a death 'ere afore the twelve-month is out.' Then Mam began to cry, and Tod told me afterwards it was because Grammam meant that she felt she'd be the one to die. So, what with one thing and another, this year had been better than most in the dead time after Christmas, and now plough-witching night had come at last, and with it perhaps, Old Oamy.

'Good evening Mr. Edwards' came the deep, ringing voice we recognised. 'I trust I see you well?'

This was what made Old Oamy so special. He looked like a tramp, and in most ways he lived like a tramp, but he certainly didn't speak like one. If you couldn't see him but could only hear him speaking, you might have thought he was a parson, or a doctor, or perhaps the person he most sounded like to us was Colonel Evison, up at the Hall in next village. There were other things different about him, though, as well. For one thing, all tramps were regarded as fair game by the children in our village (except Tod and me). But when they ran after Oamy and called him names he never turned round and swore at them or raised his stick to them as the other tramps did. He simply walked on without even turning his head, and his blue eyes – just the colour of the forget-me-nots we gathered down the dike-sides, Tod said – never lost their far-away look. The children might just as well not have been there, even when they dared each other to run up and touch him, or pull at his old sacks to try to get them off.

As I said, Tod and I never tried it, because we weren't allowed to. Dad had explained that tramps were people, just

7

like us, and if they chose to wander about without proper food or clothes they had just as much right to do it as we had to eat when we were hungry or go to bed when we were tired. On the other hand, if they didn't choose, but were forced to sleep under hedges and live on crusts, we ought to be glad that we had a good home and good food. We could be sorry for them, but we couldn't be rude.

When Dad talked to us like that, and asked us not to do things, we obeyed without question, because somehow we always wanted to please him. (We did what Mam said too, but for a different reason. She laid the law down, and we knew she meant what she said. We didn't dare risk disobeying Mam.) But in any case, neither Dad nor Mam was needed to stop us tormenting Old Oamy. We didn't ever want to do anything to him except to listen to him, for he was the most wonderful teller of tales.

He always came round to our village about twice a year, and had been doing so for two or three years by the time I'm telling you about. I remember very well the first time he ever came. It was just after harvest and I had gone out with Dad after tea to look round the stack-yard, for in those days the corn was all brought in from the fields and stacked till the steam threshing machines could come and thresh the grain out. As we came round the back of the last big stack, there was Oamy, sitting in the sunshine on the step of our big barn.

He was not a very welcome sight, and Dad was just going to give him his marching orders or 'haux 'im off', as he would have said, when the tramp got up. My Dad was a tall man, but Oamy was taller by a head; and when he spoke, his voice rolled out from his throat so deep and rich, it made me think of the sea in the picture of a beach on a South Sea island, that was in one of my books. (Tod said afterwards that she could feel Oamy's voice with the tips of her fingers, as she used to our grandmother's best black velvet cape.)

He came towards Dad, and most politely asked if there was a pump anywhere in the yard from which he could get a drink of water. Well, it wasn't like our Dad to deny anybody anything he was asked for in the proper way, and the poor old chap wasn't asking much. So Dad led the way to the pump the farm men used to fill the animals' drinking troughs from, and the tramp filled a little tin mug and took a long drink. Then he began to pull off his old clothes and started to unroll a bundle he had been carrying. I kept hold of Dad's hand while I watched, wondering what could be in it, but the tramp was very quick and clever and didn't let us see anything except what he had taken out of it. That was a roll of yellow oilskin, and when he opened it, it turned out to contain nothing more exciting than a comb and a bar of hard yellow soap. So Dad and me both understood that we were watching something a bit out of the ordinary, a tramp who knew that water could be used for other things than drinking. When Dad actually believed the tramp meant to have a wash, he sent me back to the house and told him that if he really meant to have a good scrub-up, he'd be delighted to pump on him.

It was about half an hour later that Dad came back to the house, bringing the tramp with him. Tod had her very first sight of him like that, and I could hardly believe my eyes. In spite of his ragged old clothes he looked just like any other man now, only cleaner than most. As I've told you, he was very tall, and lean rather than thin. His face was long and narrow, what you could see of it. He had a lot of thick white hair that hung down on his shoulders and a wavy beard to match, that started right up under his blue eyes and ended nearly in his waistline. Now that he had washed it, it really was almost as white as snow, and he had combed it all out, but the ends were already beginning to curl again. Dad told us afterwards how he had completed his toilet by cutting and cleaning his nails, and how he'd noticed what beautiful long, slender fingers the old man had.

When they came up to the back door, Dad opened it and called out 'Mam – have you got a bit o' grub this poor old chap can have?'

9

Mam was always generous, specially with food, so she went and made two sandwiches with bread like doorsteps and a thick hunk of cheese in the middle. She went outside to hand them to the tramp, but when he took them from her he sort of bowed to her, and thanked her so courteously that she felt quite confused, and said afterwards that all she could think of was that she wished she'd cut them a lot thinner and put ham in them instead of cheese. What she did was to order me to carry our old comfortable elbow-chair out on to the doorway for him to sit in while he ate his food, and while she made him a cup of tea.

So he sat down, and Tod and me sat on the doorstep and looked at him. Dad was leaning up against the dairy door, and soon the old man began to talk to him, while we listened with shivers running down our backs every time the tramp raised his beautiful voice. He told us about walking in the hills, which he loved. He described Wales and Scotland, and though Tod and I had never really seen a hill, we imagined the mist and the heather, and the sheep and the deer, until it almost seemed as if we were walking with him, till it began to get dark. Then all of a sudden he said he was very tired and asked Dad if he could sleep in the barn where we'd found him.

Well, I could see that Dad was in what we should call a mizzy-mozzy, which means that he didn't know what to say. He was such a kind sort of chap that he couldn't bear to say no; but we all knew far too much about tramps and vagabonds who crept into farmyards to sleep, and made off in the early morning with everything they could carry. Besides only the year before, a farmer in the next village had lost everything, his house, his buildings and all his harvest in a fire that had been caused by a tramp sneaking into his yard to sleep, and smoking. He'd dropped a fag-end, they said, and it had smouldered along until it reached dry straw, but by that time the tramp had left and was miles away.

Dad took his cap off and scratched his head while he considered it. Then he consented, 'on conditions', as he said. His conditions were that the tramp would agree to be locked in the barn all night, till Dad let him out in the morning, and that he should open his bundle for our inspection, to make sure he hadn't got any matches in it.

The old man looked troubled then, and even I could see he was not very willing. At last he said that he had no objection at all to being locked in the barn, but he would be grateful if Dad did not insist on his opening the bundle.

This made Dad suspicious. What could he have in there that it mattered about anyone seeing? Something stolen from another house or farm?

'Please yourself,' Dad said. 'There's plenty of other hedges and hovels about besides mine. It don't matter to me where you sleep, but it won't be on my land except on my conditions.' And he began to walk towards the kitchen door, to show that he meant what he said.

So the tramp gave in, and began to undo his bundle. There wasn't much in it really. There was a hunk of dry bread, and a folded red handkerchief; a small clasp-knife and the oilskin roll containing, as we knew, his comb and soap. And there was one more thing, a little box made of leather, nearly black and shiny where it had been handled, but you could see it had once been brown. It was about as big as four matchboxes stuck together, though a little deeper, and on one side edge were two small, dainty clasps. (Tod said she could see straight away that they were made of silver, but I didn't believe her.) He held his hand over the box in a protective sort of way while Dad (and all the rest of us) looked at the things he'd spread out.

'What's in that little box?' Dad asked. The tramp looked steadily back at him, with a strange sort of look in his eyes, which were as bright as a blackbird's on a sunny morning. I can only call it a proud look – or perhaps even haughty, but when he spoke his voice was as gentle and polite as ever.

'If I give you my word that it contains nothing of any in-

terest or value to anybody else but me, will you believe me?'
he said.

Dad hesitated. 'I should like to know it hadn't got fag-ends
and matches in it' he replied.

The tramp smiled, a bit ruefully. 'I've agreed to being
locked in your barn, sir' he said. 'I may not have much to live
for, but I wouldn't choose to be burnt to death in a fire of my
own making. Do you really think I'd be such a fool?'

'No – well –' said Dad, scratching his head again in his per-
plexity. 'Why not leave the little box with us in the house, all
the same?'

The old man shook his head, and began to roll up his
bundle again with a resigned but determined air. There was
no mistaking his intention. He was moving on to sleep somewhere else, under a hedge or in a ditch, but he was not going
to be parted from the leather box.

He stood up, and thanked Dad and Mam for their kindness.
'I will bid you goodnight' he said. 'I cannot oblige you by
parting with the box, even for one night, though as I said,
what is in it is of no value to anyone but me. The day I part
willingly from it will be the day I die.'

'Well, have it your own way then' said Dad. 'Sleep in the
barn, and welcome. I'll let you out when I go milking about
five o'clock tomorrow morning.' And Mam said 'And come
up to the house for some breakfast before you go.'

So Dad led the way to the barn, and Tod and I went along
as well, and saw him stowed safely for the night. We couldn't
go to sleep that night for thinking about him, and his little box,
and the 'treasure' that must be inside it. But he'd gone in the
morning before we were up, and we forgot him after a bit.

He came again about six months later and again after that.
Now, whenever he came, Mam got him a meal, and he ate it
on the doorway when it was fine and in the back wash-house
(we called 'the shed') if it was raining. Wherever he had it,
Tod and I sat on the floor close to him, and gazed at him, and
tried to get him to talk.

12

And he did. It was his way, I think, of paying us for what he had. He told us of his travels and adventures in India and Australia, Mexico and Uruguay, and parts of the world I'd never even heard of. We never knew quite whether to believe his tales or not. They always seemed to have a ring of truth, but Dad said he couldn't understand how a man could have done all he'd done in one lifetime, unless he was very rich and had no other work to do. 'Besides,' Dad said, 'he's a bit queer in the head. Not mad, I don't mean that. I mean he's got something wrong with his head that makes him act different to most folks – like the way he goes on over that box of his.'

We agreed that some parts of his tales were true, and that he believed the rest, though there was no need for us to believe it all. We disagreed about the box. I thought it had something in it, like some money, that he'd stolen somewhere. Tod was quite sure it was full of diamonds and sapphires and pearls from India, real 'treasure'. Mam thought it probably contained some old letters, and Dad said that in spite of all the old chap said, it was where he carried his 'bacca and matches.

Once, Tod plucked up her courage to ask him his name. He said he'd almost forgotten it, for he had no use now for a name; but she kept asking him, and in the end he said it. It wasn't a name we had ever heard before, and we decided we hadn't heard it properly. But Dad forbade us ever to ask him again, so we had to make the most of what we'd heard. It sounded something like 'Oamy', and after that we always called him 'Old Oamy' to each other, though never to his face.

However long the evening was, there was always one more bit of excitement for us when the time came for him to spread the contents of his bundle out for Dad's inspection before he went over to the barn to sleep. The box was always there, and he never let go of it, keeping it lovingly in his hand till he could put it back and roll the bundle up again.

Once Tod, who had got so fond of him that she'd some-times even sit where she could touch him, looked up at him and said 'Please tell Jed and me what's in your little box.' He looked at her in such a kind way that for a moment I honestly thought he was going to. He looked from her to the box, ran his fingers over the clasps, and then said 'Yes, my pretty. I'll tell you. It's a silver new nothing to wear on your sleeve.'

Now Tod and I were very disappointed, and Tod was hurt, too, and I thought she was going to cry. He was making fun of us, like all grown-ups do when they think they're being clever at our expense. We'd heard that saying about the silver new nothing all our lives. Whenever we asked what Dad was going to buy at market, or what Mam was making on her sewing machine, they would reply 'A silver new nothing to hang on your sleeve' – and it meant something special but something that you were never very likely to get.

When Oamy said it, we felt it made him more ordinary, more like other grown-ups; but since that day, we always asked him the question, and he always answered in the same way. Tod used to say wistfully, 'If we keep on asking him, he may tell us the truth one day,' but she did notice that he always said 'to *wear* on your sleeve', though Mam and Dad said 'to *hang* on your sleeve.'

'That doesn't make it any more sense' I said. 'It's a daft old saying, and I don't suppose anybody knows what it means. If it's silver, it can't be nothing.' And Tod said, 'Besides, nothing can't be new, can it? And in any case, you can't hang nothing anywhere.' And she added, 'Well, people don't wear or hang things on their sleeves, do they? It's just nonsense to put us off with.' And we had to leave it at that.

So at last we can come back to the plough-witching night I started telling you about in the first place.

'Lawks, man!' we heard Dad say. 'Come inside, out o' the wind, do. You can't be out in them rags on a night like this. Set down here, while I go and get you a hot drink and a mossel o' grub.'

The shed had been built up to the back door of the house, so you had to go through it to get outside on to the doorway. It had the big green watertank in it, and an earthenware sink, and a cooking range that was the envy of every other woman in the fen. It meant that Mam didn't have to go outside to draw water, and that she didn't have to cook on the hearth in the house-place. Dad lit the cooking range every morning when he got up, as well as the turf fire on the house-place hearth, so both rooms were always warm and cosy in winter time.

Dad had hardly got the door shut behind Old Oamy, when we heard thudding footsteps on the path down the side of the house. Grammam cocked her head on one side, and said 'Here's Jack, – a-runnin' an all. I should know his step in a million,' and sure enough, it was our Grandad. He slammed the sliding door of the shed behind him, and without taking a mite of notice of Dad and Old Oamy, blundered right through and into the house-place. Dad was just lighting a candle for Old Oamy to sit by, and he came to the house-place door with it in his hand, shielding the tiny flame with his other cupped round it. We were all gazing at Grandad, wondering whatever it could be that was causing such a hormpolodge. Grandad was a bit like Old Oamy to look at, a tall, fine figure of a man, and handsome into the bargain. Like Oamy, he had a beautiful head of snow-white hair, and a beard and moustache the same silky white. But there his resemblance to the tramp ended. Where Oamy's eyes were blue, and far-away, Grandad's were green, like gimlets. When he was in a temper, they turned red, and when he was excited, as he was now, they glinted with little red sparks, like a star on a frosty night. He was better fed than Oamy, but not much better dressed. His face beneath his ragged old cap was a dirty yellowish-white, drained of its usual ruddy colour, and made the crumpled neck handkerchief he always wore round his collarless neck seem a brighter red in comparison.

We could see there was something the matter, especially when he had to take hold of the table to keep his hands from

15

shaking. Grammam started to struggle up from the rocking chair, but sank down again with her hand to her chest. Mam got up and ran to her, while Dad hastily set the candle down in the sink, and came in. Tod and I sat glued to our chairs, watching everybody, but especially Grandad, who was trying to find his voice, and looking at Grammam.

'Meery!' he said, addressing himself over our heads to her. He always called her Meery (for Mary), though everybody else called her Poll or Polly.

'Meery! I'm seen it agin.'

Grammam opened her eyes. 'No Jack!' she said 'That you ain't! Where?'

'Just outside the gate, on the drove. In the 'edge atween here an' Shallcross's. As plain as I can see you a-settin' there! An' it looked at me out o' its grut eyes, as if it wa' just a-stan'un' there waitun' for me to see it.'

'What?' said Dad 'D'you mean as you're seen a haunt, or something?'

'Tha's just it, Bill' said Grandad, sitting down all of a sudden in Dad's chair. 'I am, true as I set 'ere! I seen the Black Dug!' (Dogs were always called 'dugs' like pigs were called 'ugs'. We understood what he meant alright. I felt the hair prickling at the back of my neck and Tod put out her hand under the tablecloth and clutched mine.)

Grandad went on. 'I'm seen it once afore, this year, outside our 'ouse.' Mam was staring with horror at him, and even Dad looked as if he didn't know what to say or do. It was Grammam who brought us back to ourselves again.

'Jack!' she said, reprovingly. 'Remember the child'en.' Then she took in the rest of us, sitting up and looking more like herself than she had done since Christmas. She made a noise in her throat, a sort of clucking that she always used to Grandad when she wanted everybody to know she hadn't believed one of his tall tales.

'Ah, I recollect' she said 'an if I remember rightly, it were when you were a-comin' 'ome late after being all day at *The*

Golden Drop! It's a wonder you di'n't see Old Nick hisself, the state you were in that night!'

'Well, I ain't bin nowheer near *The Golden Drop* this time, I'm come straight 'ome from work, an' I tell yer, I'm seen it ag'in!' He dropped his voice to a whisper, and said 'The Black Dug allus brings death in its tracks. There'll be a death 'ere afore the twelve-month's out. You mark my words!'

Mam smoothed Grammam's hair with her hand, and pulled the old green shawl closer round her mother's shoulders. She loved her mother a lot, and all of us could see that if anybody was going to die, it was most likely to be Grammam.

But Dad had recovered himself, and took the situation in hand. 'Pull yerself together, do' he said to Grandad. 'It were nothing worse than your own shadow, I'll be bound.'

Mam dried her eyes, and said hopefully 'Anyway, it were between here and Shallcross's. How do we know it wasn't meant for them? P'raps it's old Granny Ellerkin it's come to fetch.'

Dad shot her a look that made her quail, frowning to stop her saying any more in front of us. 'Don't be so silly, Mam' he ordered. 'You ought to know different. Now – what can I get this poor old fellow out here to eat? He must have something afore I take him out to the barn. An' 'adn't you better get your father something afore he goes home? Jed and Tod, if you want to speak to Jimmy's brother Ted, you'd better go and have a word now, afore you start getting ready. You'll 'ev to put some warm clo'es on under your garb, I reckon, else you'll be perished. It's dark now, but the moon'll be up afore long.' He bustled us out, and we went into the shed to speak to Old Oamy. But even Dad couldn't take the horrors away from us as quick as that. I could still feel goose pimples all down my arms, and Tod said she felt as if she'd got splinters of ice all down her backbone. As we left the house-place, I heard Grammam say 'Bill's right, Jack. But in any case it's only the second warning. O'ems allus go in threes. If it is meant for us, there'll be another afore long. I'm alright, my gel, now. I only felt a bit faint-like, seeing yer father come in like that. Can't you find him something to eat? He's famished, I'll warrant.'

Old Oamy sat warming his long lean hands by the embers of the grate. We stood in front of him, awed and a bit shy in his company, as we always were. He had heard all that had passed, and seemed to know how we felt. His voice was very gentle and soothing in its velvety sound.

'It has always been the same' he said 'and perhaps it always will be. Country folk see signs of death all round them, because death is all round them. The trees die, and the plants die. Animals die, and people die, all the time. Don't take what your grandfather said as truth, though he believes it. He is afraid he must lose the person who props up his life – it is his fear of losing your grandmother that makes him imagine black dogs out of shadows. It is his way of preparing himself to meet the blow when it does come, that's all.'

We partly understood him. Tod said 'Don't you believe in o'ems, then?'

'Omens' he corrected her, almost without thinking. 'I suppose everyone does, a bit. But it does depend on the omens! I don't believe in black dogs or white cats or headless bodies, if that's what you mean. Don't be frightened, my pretty one. Death isn't so bad if you look him straight in the eye. Remember what the poet said "Cowards die many times before their death; the valiant never taste of death but once."'

He had forgotten us, we could see. He was gazing into the fire, with his far away look back in his blue eyes, and went on mumbling under his breath. I thought he was praying out loud, like Grammam always did; but Tod was closer to him than me, and she said he was 'saying po'try' like we had to at school, though she couldn't understand it. It was Tod who remembered what I've written down, and she swears that's what he said, but I don't know. It sounded grand when he said it, and that was enough for Tod. She always did love grand words.

It was Tod, though, who brought us back to the present on this occasion. She had glanced back into the house-place, and caught sight of the grandfather clock that had belonged to our dad's grandfather.

'Jed!' she said. 'Come on! We shall be LATE!' The urgency in her voice roused Old Oamy from his mumbling.

'Late for what?' he asked.

'Plough-witching!' Tod answered, in such a tragic voice that the tramp and I both laughed. Tod didn't care, this time.

She pulled me behind her through the house-place and into the lobby at the bottom of the stairs, where we had been allowed to leave our things all ready.

Within five minutes we went back into the house-place again. I was now wearing one of Mam's long skirts, tied up as high as I could get it under my arms, and an old shirt of Dad's cut down to make me a waist (blouse) to tuck into it. I had one of Grammam's hats on, from which some straggly bits of shaggy black horse hair were draped round my face.

Tod had a pair of my knickerbockers on, which were a lot too long for her, so that they came nearly down to her ankles; and over the top of them she wore a soldier's red coat, buttons and all, that was so big that she looked absolutely ridiculous, especially with her long fair plaits hanging down over each shoulder. But when our other grandmother had bought it for a shilling to put a red pattern in her pegged rug, Tod had pleaded so hard to be allowed to keep it for plough-witching that Dad had given his mother a shilling to get another with. Mam didn't peg rugs, and I guessed that Grandmother knew she would get it back in time. I knew her well enough to know that Dad wouldn't get his shilling back, though.

All the rest of the family looked at us and laughed when we went in as we had known they would. Dad was sitting by Oamy's candle, holding a cork in the flame. Tod went to him and stood waiting expectantly.

He took the cork from the flame, let it cool, and then blacked Tod's face with it, all over, except for a little patch round each eye. Then he put the cork in the flame again and attended to my face in the same way. He took hold of Tod's plaits, and lifted them up. Without saying a word he got up and went to where Mam was sitting, and drew some hairpins from the great bun of hair at the back of her neck. With these, he pinned Tod's plaits on top of her head, and from his jacket pocket took a little fur cap. With this addition to her garb, and without her hair, I shouldn't have recognised her at all. Dad had wheedled the fur cap out of Uncle John for Tod, and kept it as a surprise. I knew there'd be one for me as well – not a fur cap, I mean a surprise of some sort. I wasn't wrong. Dad went into the corner of the shed, where some old sacks were lying. From underneath them he produced the biggest and best turnip lantern I'd ever seen. It was made of a huge mangold, with all the middle scooped out, and a face cut into one side. There were strings to carry it by, and a candle bedded in its own wax stood in the bottom, ready for lighting.

We went to be inspected once again. Grammam said 'Well, I declare! Your own mother wouldn't know you! Keep your mouth shut, Jed, and nobody'll guess you're a boy. If you carried a baby, folks would swear you were a gipsy woman, that they would.' She took off her own green wool shawl, and fastened it with a hairpin round my shoulders, while Tod picked up the precious wax doll she had had for Christmas, and put it in my arms. I said I wasn't going to carry any silly doll about, plough-witching or no plough-witching but Tod said I need only have it when we actually went into a house, because I should be carrying the lantern anyway. She could manage the tin with the hole in the top, and carry the doll till we were outside of a house.

So Dad lit the candle in the turnip lantern, and put us our first penny in the tin, to make it rattle. Then away we went, out of the shed door at the back of the house. Dad waited to see us off the doorway, holding the door open. 'No silly tricks, now' he said 'and be home here at eight o'clock, or I shall come and look for you at the top of the drove.'

He shut the door, and the thick darkness closed round us. The grinning face of our lantern gleamed horribly in the black night, for the moon hadn't got up yet. Suddenly, we were afraid. Tod came close to me, as we stopped by the end of the house, out of the biting wind, trying to get our courage up.

'Jed' said Tod in a whisper. 'What about the black dog?' She only voiced just what I was thinking. As soon as we got out of the shelter of the house, we should be on the drove by the side of the hedge that ran between our house and Shallcross's, just where Grandad had seen it. We daren't go on, but we couldn't go back and say we were scared. We didn't want to miss going plough-witching, either, now that we were all ready.

'Let's coo-ee, and see if Flossy and Sar'anne and them have gone yet' said Tod. 'If they haven't we can all go along the drove together, and then go to different houses.'

It sounded a good idea. By 'and them', Tod meant the rest of the Shallcross children, besides the twins.

We went as far as the end of the house, and called 'Coo-ee'. The answer came back from close to where we stood, two voices chanting.

> 'And when you're hid, holler,
> Else the little dogs wou'n't foller'

Then out of the hedge bottom came Floss and Sar'anne. Both of them had got pegged rugs pinned round their necks, and a bit of black stuff tied over their heads to cover up their hair, because everyone in the fen for miles around would know them straight away if they saw that hair. It was so long the girls could sit on it, and it was thick and wavy, so that little curls always escaped and stuck on their foreheads when they got hot playing a game. But what the women all went on about, and envied, was the colour of it. If it had been a little bit darker, it would have been ginger, and they could have despised it as 'carrots'. If it had been a bit lighter, it would have been just fair hair, like Tod's; but it was in between, a

21

coppery colour with red and gold lights in it, and even I could see why Mam complained as she dragged Tod's straight fair hair back into plaits. 'I wonder why you couldn't have had hair like the Shallcross gels.' Mam took being outdone by her neighbours very hard, and in the matter of the Shallcross twins' hair, there wasn't a lot she could do about it.

Floss and Sar'anne had their faces blacked, of course.

'Oo, what a lovely lantern, Tod' said Flossie to me. Tod nearly screamed with laughter because they had been taken in by our change of clothes, and thought I was Tod.

'What's the matter with your Grandad?' Sar'anne asked. 'What frit 'im?'

'What do you mean?' we said.

Floss took up the tale. 'We were ready early' she said, 'so we come out to wait till you had gone, 'cos we wanted to go to your'n first. We set down under the hedge to be out o' the wind. Then that ole tramp come, and we see 'un go into your'n.'

'M'm' put in Sar'anne, 'right inside the door. Your dad let 'im in. I seed 'im! A mucky ole tramp like 'im.' Her voice showed what she thought about such goings-on, for there wasn't another house anywhere around where Old Oamy would have been allowed as much as to set foot on the doorway. I could sense Tod bristling, ready to defend Dad and Oamy but I didn't want her to stop Floss telling her tale, so I pinched Tod's arm, and she shut up.

Floss went on. 'Then when the ole tramp had gone in your dad shut the door, and me an' Sar'anne reckoned we'd better start somewheer else, an' not at your'n, 'cos we din't want to go in while the tramp were there. But we knowed we should git a penny from your Dad, so we waited agin. Then we heard somebody comin' along the path a-singin', and we guessed it were your grandad. We were a sight worse frit o' Rattles than we were o' the tramp, an' we stood still against the 'edge, so's 'e shou'n't see us. An' then just as he were a-goin' by us, he yelped out loud an' started to run.'

22

'I said as 'ow 'e might a-bin took short, an' 'ad to run to the closet,' Sar'anne put in. 'But 'e di'n't go down the path to it — he run right inside the shed door, and slammed it to.'

I heard Tod gasp, as if she'd been stung, so I lifted the lantern up to look at her face. I couldn't tell whether she was about to laugh or cry, but the light from the lantern fell on the twins as well as on Tod, and I suddenly saw what Tod had worked out. The Black Dug was standing there in front of us, only it had four white eyes instead of two. Grandad hadn't told us that. I could see that Tod was going to burst out laughing in a minute, and I didn't want to waste any more plough-witching time explaining. So I said to Floss and Sar'anne 'You can go to our house now. The tramp's only having some tea' and Tod said 'Yes, we're going to Aunt 'Loll's first, and then on to the high road to grandmother's, afore we go anywhere else.' So we parted, and managed not to laugh until we'd got over the planks across the dyke that lay between our drove and the path to where our aunt and uncle lived. In the distance as we crossed the bendy planks by the light of our lantern, we could hear Floss and Sar'anne outside our shed door, singing 'Just one! Just one! Just one for the poor old ploughboy! Just one! Just one!' and shaking their tin, that we knew had so far only got a little stone in it, to make it rattle.

We went on till we came to a little bridge across the drain, and along the road till we got to the cottage our Aunt 'Loll lived in. When she'd got married to Uncle Jim, they'd gone away to live, and they hadn't been back in the fen very long. We didn't know them really very well yet, but we always loved Uncle Jim. In any case, though, we had been told that Aunt Harriet and Uncle John, from right across the turf-fen, were coming up to Aunt 'Loll's tonight to see the fun. There'd be a lot o' grown-up folks out plough-witching later on, when all us children were gone home again.

Outside Aunt 'Loll's door we shook our tin, and began to call 'Just one! Just one!' When the latch on the door began to click, Tod remembered, and pushed her doll into my arms.

23

We could see right into the house when the door opened, and sure enough there was Uncle John sitting beside the hearth, and our aunts sat at the table. Uncle Jim held the door open, so the others could see us.

'Let's hear you sing then' said Uncle Jim. So I held the lantern up with one hand, and hugged the doll with the other, while Tod rattled the tin as we struck up the ploughboy's song.

> 'Hole in your stocking, hole in your shoe
> Please will you give me a penny or two.
> If you ain't got a penny, a ha'penny'll do
> And if you ain't got a ha'penny,
> Well God-bless-you!'

'Just one! Just one! Just one! Just one!'

'Come on in, there's good child'en' Aunt Harriet called out. 'That there ol' wind don't want no invitation, wi' the door open like that.'

So we went in, and by the light of the oil lamp they all looked us up and down and tried to guess who we were, asking us questions to trap us into answering so that they should know our voices. But Tod and I had been plough-witching before, and knew better than to say anything except 'Just one'.

Aunt 'Loll brought out some mince pies and plum cake, and we ate in silence while they kept on trying to guess our names. Uncle Jim was attending to a pot that hung over the turf fire, and the smell that came from it told me it was elderberry wine being hotted up, ready for the ginger and sugar. At home, Mam would be hotting up brown ale and mixing it with sugar and ginger and eggs, and putting in a drop of brandy. It was a lovely drink when you came in cold after plough-witching, though of course us children weren't supposed to have it (though we sometimes did, for a bad cold on the chest). Old Oamy, I thought, would get a good mugful before he went out to the barn. It was lucky for him he'd come on this night of the year, when everybody had something hot and spicy simmering on the hob. When Uncle Jim bent over the pot, Uncle John gave me a broad wink, to let me know that he had recognised us, but was not letting on. Of course – Tod was wearing his own fur cap, and I learned afterwards that he'd been all the afternoon helping Dad to scoop out the middle of our lantern, and fixing it up for us.

At last Aunt Harriet said 'Well, I'm sure I don't know who they are. I can see I shall have to find 'em a penny' and she fished under her apron for the pocket she wore tied round her waist. Uncle John gave us another, and Uncle Jim found two ha'pennies in his tobacco tin. Then Uncle John said to Aunt Harriet 'Well, you are a muzzle-'ead, not to know Jed and Tod when you see 'em!'

'Well, as I go to school!' Aunt Harriet exclaimed. Then she said to me 'You've growed such a big gal, Tod, it's the truth I should never a-knowed you! But I ought to have reckernised that wax doll, for there ain't another in the fen made o' wax, I'll warrant.' Then both of us burst out laughing, and Tod said 'That's Jed, Aunt Harriet, I'm Tod.'

Aunt Harriet looked us over, and we could see she was very put out at having been taken in like that. She put on her 'chapelface' and set her mouth in a line, and said no more.

We began to talk, then, and Tod started to tell Uncle John about Grandad Rattles and the black dog. She thought it would amuse them, but it had the opposite effect. I know now that it upset Aunt Harriet and Aunt 'Loll very much to be reminded that they were related by marriage to Grandad Rattles, and it seemed as if they just wouldn't listen to what we were saying, however often we explained about Floss and Sar'anne being in the hedge. They kept on talking as if Grandad really had seen The Black Dog.

'Poor old gal' Aunt 'Loll said. 'She's been ailing a goodish while now. I should think it's a cancer, 'cos she used to be a real bonny woman once.'

'Yes' nodded Aunt Harriet 'though I reckon she never gets enough to eat. That old rapscallion never did do a day's work, an' never will. He'll miss her, though, when she's gone, but I'm sure it'll be a happy release for her.'

They were talking about our Grammam, of course, burying her already because of the silly black dog.

I said 'Aunt Harriet, there wasn't a dog. It was only Flossie and Sar'anne Shallcross dressed up.' She ignored me, but said to Aunt 'Loll, 'You can't laugh such o'ems off. I know as Bill allus tries to, like when he see the white cat. But it were that very week arter Bill see the cat that cousin Hosea died over at Raveley. That were a blood relation, of course, 'cos Hosea were let's see – 'e'd be our mother's cousin's oldest daughter's son – the one she 'ad – you know.' (She had dropped her voice to a whisper.)

Uncle John said 'Lawks, Harriet how you do go on! It's years since Bill see that ole white cat up on the high road outside Tommydod's place. It were afore he were married, 'cos my brother Will were with him. Nobody ain't seen that haunt for donkey's years.'

'No, but that's no reason why they shou'n't, is it? I'll lay if anybody does, they'll lose somebody kin to 'em, or somebody under the same roof, afore the year's out.'

I nudged Tod, and said we had better be going, because we were going up to Grandmother's, and then to the Commonbridge, and then to Uncle George's, and then to Uncle Herb and Aunt Sis, before we went home. (They were the only houses Dad would let us go to. Uncle George and Aunt Rose, and Uncle Herb and Aunt Sis, were no relation to us, but friends of Mam and Dad, and their children out ploughwitching would come to our house in return. Dad wouldn't let us go anywhere where they were too poor to spare us a ha'penny.)

So we got to the door before Aunt Harriet spoke to us again. 'And don't you ever let me see you wearing boy's clothes again' she said in her sternest voice to Tod. 'It is a wicked thing to do and I'm surprised that a brother of mine should ever allow such a sin in his family. But there, what can you expect, from one o' that old scoundrel's kin!'

We were absolutely flabbergasted at this turn of events, and I could see Tod was going to answer her back if I didn't do something quick and then the fat would be in the fire. So I pinched Tod, and said 'Why is it wicked, Aunt Harriet? We didn't know.' Aunt Harriet got her mouth ready in her chapellest face, and said, 'It's an abomination unto the Lord. It says so in the Bible.'

Then we were outside again, in the dark, with only the tiny glow of our candle lantern.

Tod didn't cry, because she was too angry. She stamped her foot on the old brick doorway, and stuck her tongue out as far as it would go in Aunt Harriet's direction, and said 'I hate you, Aunt Harriet. You're a bomination unto the Lord, an' a bitch an' all. I hate you, and I hate the dratted ol' Bible, so there!'

I was aghast, and waited for Tod to be struck by lightning, or something just as bad. Mam and Grandmother were always telling us that God was watching us every minute, and could tell if we ever even thought anything wicked. And here was Tod, dressed up in boy's clothes and saying out loud that she hated the Bible. I couldn't see how God could pretend he hadn't heard, so he'd have to punish Tod somehow.

'Tod!' I said, when I could get my breath back 'Say your prayers, quick.'

Not Tod. She stuck her chin out, and grabbed her precious doll out of my arms, and stumped off towards the stile that led out to the high road. I let her go, while I stood on Aunt 'Loll's doorway and said 'Our Father' and 'Lighten our darkness, we beseech Thee O Lord', because although that was a church prayer and we went to chapel, we had to say it every day at school before we set off home, so it must be alright. Besides, it seemed to fit the occasion better than 'Gentle Jesus', which was the only other prayer I could say. I felt

27

better when I'd said it, anyhow, and just as I started to run after Tod as well as I could with the long skirt flapping round my boots, the clouds parted and the full moon came out. I thought my prayer had been answered, but it made me all the more sure God must have heard Tod, and I thought that if he didn't punish her in some way or other, I should never believe Mam or Grandmother again.

I was dreading going to Grandmother's now, because she was as set on the Bible as Aunt Harriet. But she was in a real good mood, and had some home-made toffee waiting for us, besides giving us two ha'pennies. We began to cheer up, and enjoy our plough-witching again. We visited our two other houses, and then set off by the long way round home, to call at the Commonbridge, where one of Dad's old friends lived. When we got there, we were asked into the kitchen, which was already so full of people that we could hardly get in. There was a big family there, all grown up, and every one of them was there in the kitchen. Sitting by the side of the hearth, as well, was Simmy Rouncer. He was nearly as old as our dad, but was only a little taller than me, and had a humped back. He was queer in the head, as well, and had fits sometimes. He loved to visit other people's houses, and sit by their fires, because nobody took much notice of him at home. He often came to our house, and both Mam and Dad told us we must never tease him or be rude to him, in case he had a fit. He'd just come and sit by the fire, like he was doing to-night at the Commonbridge, and make a remark now and again that seemed to show he wasn't half as silly as folks said he was.

We stood on the hearthrug and sang our song, and all the family pretended they didn't know us, and guessed wrong, just to please us. Then all of a sudden, Simmy jumped up, and said in his funny way of speaking 'S'e's a b'ack faced woman wid a white baby. That ain't right, is it?' and before I could move he'd snatched Tod's beautiful wax doll out of my arms, and pushed it up the chimney, over the top of the fire, to black its face in the soot. Tod screamed, and all the family jumped to the rescue. One of them pulled the doll away from Simmy – but it was too late. The fair hair was clogged with soot and her pretty face and clothes all blackened. Worst of all, the wax had melted from her nose and cheeks, so that she looked quite horrid. Tod began to wail and cry, cuddling the doll and kissing it. The woman of the house led Tod to the sink in the corner, to try to put some of the damage right, while the father said angrily 'Simmy, you shou'n't a-done that there! Whatever come over you to make you do such a wicked thing?'

After that, it was such a to-do that I almost forgot what happened next. Simmy began to make queer noises, and froth came out all round his mouth, and then he fell out of his chair on to the hearthrug. Some of the family screamed, and some yelled to tell the others what to do, and everybody rushed from one side of the tiny kitchen to the other and got in each other's way. Somebody pushed me and Tod outside and told us to go home, which we did, as fast as we could, with Tod still sobbing over her spoilt doll.

Our candle had burnt out, because we were later than we ought to have been; but the clouds had broken up a good deal, and the full moon made our way quite clear to see. We were still on the high road, our boots rattling and crunching, and occasionally even striking sparks from the huge lumps of loose granite with which it had recently been made up. We were still a long way from the top of our drove, and getting tired. We were quiet now, because the accident with Tod's doll had taken the fun out of our evening. I kept thinking all the time that God had let Tod off real light, and hoped there wasn't any more punishment to come, at least till we got home. But the silence between us seemed unnatural, and I began to think about all sorts of things I really didn't want to think about at all, like The Black Dog and other haunts as I'd heard about.

Then I remembered Aunt Harriet going on about The

White Cat, because that was a new one to me, but it seemed from what they'd said that our Dad had actually seen it, once. And I was still thinking about it when I realised we were on the very stretch of road Aunt Harriet had mentioned. I didn't know whether to say anything to Tod or not. She had stopped sobbing, and was looking all round her in the moonlight, turning from side to side. The road shone out in front of us, sparkling as the moon caught the granites. On each side of the road, the wide grass verge sloped downwards to the dykes, and beyond the dykes on each side the fen stretched away, it seemed for ever. There were a few houses scattered here and there, with the lamplight shining out of the windows, but none close at hand by the roadside. Just ahead of us was a five barred gate standing open and inside the gate, the other side of the sleeper bridge that spanned the dyke, was a hovel where the smallholder kept a few of his implements. The inside of the hovel was in shadow, but we'd been by it enough times in the daylight to know exactly what was in it.

Tod quickened the pace, and I knew without her telling me that she'd thought of Aunt Harriet's tale, as well. Then she stopped, and clutched my arm, gasping for breath.

'Jed' she said, in a terrible whisper that frightened me of its own accord '*There it is!*'

I looked where she was looking, and sure enough, from the side of the dyke a white creature was moving. We stopped dead in our tracks, clinging to each other, as the animal lifted itself clear of the dyke side and moved silently across the grass. It was a sleek but fair-sized cat, as purposeful as cats hunting at night always are. It took no notice of us at all, but came out on to the road in front of us, picking its way among the stones, and crossed to the other side, over the verge, and down into the other dyke.

I felt the hair at the back of my neck rising, and put my hand up to it. Of course, I was still wearing Grammam's old hat, though I'd quite forgotten my plough-witching garb. I don't know what would have happened next, if we had truly

30

been alone after the cat disappeared. As it was, there was a whistle from the hovel in front of us. Tod called out in terror, but while I froze on the spot and thought I was going to faint with fright, she began to run as fast as her clothes would let her, and threw herself at the figure that had come out of the hovel. Next minute, Dad was kneeling on the road with his arms round both of us while we sobbed out our tale, because I could cry as well now that we were safe.

Dad had come to look for us when it began to get late. He'd heard us coming along the road, and taken shelter from the wind till we reached him. He'd been watching us in the moonlight, and had seen us stop and cling to each other – but he hadn't seen the White Cat.

He tried to assure us that it was only a flesh and blood cat out prowling, but we didn't believe him because we knew he didn't believe himself. As we set off home again, one each side of him, he said 'Do you think you can keep it a secret, what you saw? It would only upset Mam and Grammam. Can we have a secret between the three of us, and never tell nobody, not ever? Will you try to do that, to please me?'

We said we would – and a very difficult thing it was to keep that promise, but we did. So Grammam never did know that the third warning had come. Tod and I talked about it at nights, when we were safe in our beds; and we had our hearts in our mouths every time Grammam got the wind, or felt a bit faint, or complained of a pain in her foot. We didn't want her to die and leave us, and we were frightened at the thought of death in our house. We'd forgotten what Old Oamy had said about it.

He'd gone into the barn when we reached home, and the damage to Tod's doll occupied all the rest of us. Mam got some warm water and cleaned the doll up; the damage to her nose and cheeks was not as bad as it might have been, and Tod said she loved her better than ever because she'd been hurt by the fire. We got to bed at last, with plough-witching over for another year. We were dog-tired, and fell asleep almost at once. I decided not to tell anybody what Tod had said about hating the Bible, hoping God would forget it as well. He was the only person besides me who knew what she'd done, and if He didn't split on her, I wasn't going to.

SHE CRACKS, SHE BEARS; SHE BENDS, SHE BREAKS

NEXT MORNING, THE wind had dropped, and it had begun to snow in earnest. Mam tried to get Old Oamy to stop in our barn, but he wouldn't. He set off into the snow, wearing one of Dad's old coats over his sacks, and we watched him stride off, taking no more notice of the weather than he would have done if the sun had been shining. His little bundle hung from a stick over his shoulder, bigger than usual with the food Mam had packed up for him. I said so, to Tod. She nodded, and said 'And the little box is in it, as well, with the silver new nothing. I wonder if he'll ever tell us what's really inside?'

It snowed, and it snowed, and it snowed. We couldn't go to school, and Grammam couldn't go home. January was coming to an end. Grammam said 'Feery-weery fill dyke, either black or white' and we all laughed, because we had heard the joke many a time about the old couple who kept *The Spade and Shovel*. On the last day of January, the old man had said 'Another month gone, and tomorrow's the fust o' Feery-weery.'

'Silly old fool, you' his wife had replied. 'Lived all these year an' still can't say Febry-webry.'

It was white nearly till the end of February, and then the thaw set in, and where there had been snow, there was now water. The dykes and drains couldn't deal with it fast enough, and then the bank of the river blowed, and hundreds of acres of fen were flooded, especially the low bit between the river and the main drain. It was just a sheet of water stretching away as far as you could see into the distance, with only a reed or two sticking out here and there, as bleak as it could ever be.

Tod and me were praying as hard as we could every night, quite forgetting that God had reason not to listen to Tod's prayers. We wanted it to freeze again and only God could arrange that. We told Dad we were praying for a frost so we could go skating, but he looked worried at the thought, and said it was all right for us, but what about all the children whose dads hadn't been able to go to work because of the snow, and now because of the flood. If a long frost set in, they would be crying with cold and hunger, and their mothers would have to tell them Jack Frost had frez the cupboard doors up. We felt sorry for them if it was so; but we still prayed for a frost, and God heard our prayer.

Within a week, what had been a sea of water was now a sheet of ice, as smooth and flawless as grey-green glass. Then out came the skating pattens, and a lot of swapping went on between families if the children had grown out of the ones that had fitted their boots the year before. Then the straps had to be softened, or sometimes replaced altogether, and the blades ground to get a good edge on them. Last of all, we had to sit without our boots while Dad drilled a hole in the heel of each one for the screw of the patten to fit into. Dad got his own and Mam's skates ready as well, and Grandad came and brought his for Dad to see to, and a pair of women's for Dad to get ready in case our Aunt Lizzie came, because she was a very pretty skater and would come for a few days if it was at all possible.

Grandad was a lovely skater as well, strong and handsome but with such a delicate way of picking his feet up that folks who wouldn't look the way he was on in the ordinary way stopped to watch him, and tell him what a picture he made. He had his eye to business, of course. After the first few days, when the folk who lived in the fen had the ice almost to them- selves, the visitors would start to arrive. There'd be crowds of young folks, walking from Ramsey if they didn't happen to be very good skaters, with their pattens hanging over their shoulders. Those who were confident just got on to the nearest dyke or drain and followed it till they skated all the way to the great sheet of ice over the flood. There, everybody was safe, because it was only about eighteen inches deep, and frozen nearly solid. The better-off would arrive on bicycles, or with a pony and trap; and at last would come the parties from the Big Houses – Sir John with his family and friends, and others like him, sometimes driving in a carriage and four with a real coachman up in front. It was the only time I ever remember really seeing a coach and four, because they were going out of fashion just about this time, but I do remember people arriving once or twice in that grand way.

As soon as this invasion started, Grandad would give up skating for his own pleasure, and look to making as much money out of the situation as he could. He'd take a chair with him down to the ice, and his tools, and there he'd stand, waiting to put other folk's pattens on for them, at sixpence a time. The ladies and gentlemen would sit on the chair while Rattles knelt in front of them fixing their pattens with screws and tightening the straps. Then he would help them up, steadying them till they found their balance on their skates. He'd doff his old cap to the ladies, and offer them his arm till they were ready to strike out, sometimes even crossing hands with them and skating a few yards with them side by side, till they got going. Then he'd leave go and made a wide circle crossing one foot over in front of the other, as graceful as a bird, before he lunged forward and got back to his chair in one stroke, ready for the next customer. All over the ice, as far as you could see, there were people skating. The youngest children, hardly more than babies, all wrapped up with scarves and shawls till they looked like roly-poly puddings just coming out of the pot, were learning to go for the first time on tiny pattens only four or five inches long. Their mams and dads would have brought a little low chair for them, and the babies were left to find out how to skate by pushing the chair in front of them to keep them from falling over. Of course, children as old as Tod and me could all skate as well as we could walk, but we were told to keep well to the side, so as not to get in the way of the grown-ups. The real ladies and gentlemen would be going sedately up and down, by themselves or in couples. The ladies skating alone looked beautiful, with their hands in fur muffs and backs as straight as wheat straw. The gentlemen folded their arms very often, and nearly leaned backwards to show themselves off; but quite often they would pair off with a lady, give hands across, and strike out together. I used to stop and watch Dad skating with Aunt Lizzie like this, and think they looked better than any of the gentry from Ramsey or Upwood. But this kind of skating was very different from the sort the real fenmen like Grandad and his mates did. They went in for speed skating, and raced each other, travelling like the wind across the field of ice into the distance. Once they got going, they leaned forward and swung their arms with each stroke – and woe betide any other skater who got in their way. They would be practising in case the frost lasted long enough for any proper races to be set up on The Delph, or on Bury Fen, with money prizes. And Grandad would be telling everybody how when he was a young man he'd skated a mile faster than ever Fish Smart or Turkey Smart did (which of course was a lie, but nobody could contradict him). And sometimes a whole gang of young men would get going together, not side by side, but one behind the other, each taking hold of the one in front of him, and striking out in unison, with the best skater in front to set the pace, and another experienced man at the back because the tail sometimes swung about. Now and again such a line would be tripped up, and the whole lot would fall and spin about in a heap, while the onlookers clapped and laughed at them.

Everybody took food and drink with them, and when there was a full moon they went home to get warm and have a meal, and then out again to skate by moonlight, though of course children had to go home as soon as it began to get dusk, and their mothers left the ice as well, to go and put them to bed and to prepare supper for the men when they finally got home.

Ah, it was lovely to live in the old fen when a frost set in after a flood. It's a pleasure nobody knows these days, since the new ways of draining keep the fen from being flooded. Skating on a river or a drain is alright, but it isn't the same as having a square mile of ice as you know is nearly solid under your feet. On a river or a drain, there would always be a few weak places where somebody had kept breaking the ice to dip water for the house or farm. When the dipping holes got frez over, they made skating dangerous, because if you got in under the thick ice there wasn't much hope for you. Nobody could help you because if they came over towards you the ice round the edges of the hole broke away with their weight. If there didn't happen to be a pole or a clothes prop handy, there wasn't much anybody could do.

Of course, after the first day or two, the ice would be criss-crossed all over with marks made by the blades, and it soon lost its look of being greeny-coloured glass. The most marks would be round the edges, because that's where all the chil-dren and the folk that couldn't skate very well, would be. The old men whose skating days were over would stand together on the river bank, and talk about what they could do when they were young, as well as criticise all the skaters spread out in front of them like a picture. And every now and then the ice would crack right across with a sound like a gun going off. Then folks as didn't know any better would fly to the side, and shriek because they thought they were going to be let into the water – especially the fine ladies and the young dink-me-dolls from Ramsey as had only come to show off.

The old men on the bank would laugh and slap the sides of their drabbette trousers, and call to us children.

'You're orl roight, me little ol' ducks. She cracks, she bears: she bends, she breaks.'

We knew it was the truth, too. The ice round a dipping hole always felt as if it was bending.

Well, we were able to skate that year I'm telling you about. The ice bore well by the Monday, but we had to go to school and there wasn't much time between getting home and dark, so we were all looking forward to Saturday. We knew we shouldn't be allowed to go on Sunday. We weren't allowed to do anything on Sundays except go to Sunday School and Chapel, and read The Bible or the *Life of Christ*.

On Saturday, just as we were about to set out, Old Oamy turned up again, though it was only about six weeks since he'd come before. And when we looked up the drove towards the high road to see if any of our mates were coming, we could see our Aunt Lizzie in the distance. She had come on the early train from Peterborough for a day's skating and would stop till Monday morning. It was almost too good to be true, though as Tod said, we couldn't be skating and listening to Old Oamy's stories at the same time. He slept in our barn as usual that Saturday night, though he was sitting in the shed by the grate when we went home to tea. Mam wasn't much of a skater, and after the first day or two she'd make an excuse to stop at home, so that she had a hot meal ready for the rest of us when we went in. Dad and Aunt Lizzie would go back again after tea to skate by moonlight, we knew, but we should have to go to bed. Still, as Tod said, we could talk to Old Oamy a little while first, and that almost made up for not being allowed to go back to the ice.

When we bundled through the shed door, carrying our pattens, he looked up to speak to us; and when he saw our beautiful aunt, rosy and flushed with the cold and the skating, he scrambled out of his chair and stood up to speak to her, and kept standing there in his old rags till she had gone into the house-place and out of sight again.

'Hang your pattens up' Dad said. 'You won't want 'em again till Monday night, if the frost lasts that long.'

Tod pouted, and put on her stubborn look.

'Why can't we go tomorrow?' she said. 'Silly old Sunday! I don't want to go to Sunday School.'

Dad said, quite sharply, for him. 'That's enough Tod. You know very well why we don't skate on Sundays, any more than we should have a horkey, and dance on the Lord's day.'

Tod wasn't going to give in. 'But God sends the frost' she said. 'Why doesn't he want us to enjoy it? It'll thaw before next Saturday, I'll bet.'

Dad took her pattens, and mine, and hung them over a hook high up on the wall. He wasn't going to argue with Tod, but his action shut her up just as well. No arguments or pleading would move him on that sort of thing, and we knew it.

So on the morning of Sunday we were dressed up in our best clothes and sent off to Sunday School as usual. Dad would follow later, because he was a teacher; then he'd stay on to the morning service. We were allowed to please ourselves whether we stopped to the service, or went home after Sunday School. We usually stopped, because Tod liked the singing, and both of us liked the walk home with Dad all to ourselves. But it didn't seem right to be inside when the whole fen was sparkling with rime in the winter sunshine, so we agreed to go home and not wait for Dad that day.

We set off with a lot of other children that went our way. Flossie and Sar'anne Shallcross were there, of course. They had their best clothes on which meant they had starched white pinafores, all frills, covering up their old darned frocks under their coats. The other difference from their work-a-day appearance was that they wore their beautiful hair loose. The plaits they wore to school had been undone and brushed out, so their hair fell in great coppery waves down below their waists, like cloaks, and both of them had a bit of green ribbon round their heads to keep it off their faces, and a little round hat sat on top of it.

Tod said 'You look just like the angels in our *Life of Christ* – only they didn't wear hats and pinafores. I wish I had hair like yours.'

Floss said. 'You kin 'ev it, for all I care. Dratted ol' 'air. It don't 'alf pull when Mam brushes it out' and Sar'anne added 'Ah! you wou'n't want it when Mam 'as to pour paraffin an' vinegar all over it, if she thinks she sees a nit in it.'

Tod, as usual, had the last word. 'Well, I wish I had hair that looked like angels'. I should love to be a angel.'

Floss and Sar'anne laughed. 'I'd ruther be a gal, an' goo skatin'' Floss said, and 'Loll nodded. They stopped and looked all round to see nobody else was near enough to hear.

'We 'ood our pattens last night, so's we could git 'em this morning 'uthout nobody seein' us. We're goin' skatin' now, till dinner time. Mam'll think we've stopped to chapel. Why don't you come, an' all?'

I said 'We mustn't, 'cos it's Sunday' and Sar'anne said scornfully 'I know that, silly-billy. More musn't we, but we're going to, all the same.'

Tod said, slowly 'We should have to get into the shed and steal our pattens, 'cos Dad hung 'em up last night. But I reckon Jed could reach 'em if he stood on a chair . . .'

I was no match for three girls. Perhaps I didn't really want to be, because I wanted to go skating as much as any of them. I began to waver.

'We couldn't get down to the ice an' back again by dinner time' I said. 'By the time we'd put each other's pattens on, it 'ould be time to take 'em off again.'

'Who said anything about goin' down all the way to the ice, clever?' said Floss. 'We're goin' on the Catchwater.'

I gave in. We said we'd meet them if we could get into the shed, get our pattens down and slip out without being seen. They said they'd hide in the dyke opposite to our houses for a little while, and if we didn't come they'd go without us.

We crossed the drove a goodish bit above our house, and then got down in the dyke and walked along the ice, so that Mam or Aunt Lizzie or Grammam shouldn't see us if they happened to be looking out of the front window. It led us into the garden at the blank side of the house, and we crept up the path from the lavatory, and slid the shed door gently back.

Then we stopped and listened. We were in luck. The door to the house-place was closed, and we could hear the voices of Mam, Grammam and Aunt Lizzie through it. They were 'having five minutes' of gossip round the fire, while Dad was out of the way, and we could tell how much they were enjoying themselves.

We lifted Old Oamy's chair from beside the grate, so that it shouldn't scrape on the floor tiles, and carried it across to the wall. Then I got in it, and unhooked our pattens from among the rest. We put the chair back, and went out again the way we had come. I'd begun to enjoy the adventure, by this time, and pushed out of my head any thoughts about what Dad would say if he knew. As far as I could see, he need never know. It was still only a little past eleven, and there was a full hour and a half before he'd be home. I made up my mind that I should have to try and judge the time, and pull Tod away by force if she wouldn't come willingly when I said so.

We were all giggling and silly with excitement when we joined Floss and Sar'anne crouching in the dyke. We crept along it, bent double, till we got far enough away from the houses. Then we ran along the top of it till it joined the Catchwater, and there, free from all eyes, we climbed up on to the bank to sit down and put our pattens on.

When we'd scrambled to the top of the bank, we saw him. Old Oamy was sitting in the sun on the Catchwater side of the bank, all among the rimey grass, eating a sandwich of bread and meat our Mam had given him before he left that morning. His long lean hands were as clean as our own, and he had paused in his munching to stare into the distance, like he so often did, with his blue eyes looking far away at nothing.

We stopped dead at the sight of him, all bunched up together on the top of the bank.

Then Floss and Sar'anne spoke, as they so often did, together, so that you never really knew which of them had said what.

'It's on'y that mucky ol' tramp, agin. We nee'n't take no notice o'r'im.' And they sat down and began to struggle with the straps of their skates.

Oamy looked, startled by the voices. Then he saw us, and shook his head as if to clear his eyes, and make sure he wasn't dreaming. He put down his sandwich in the grass and got to his feet.

'Jed!' he said 'and you too Tod? What are you doing here?' Tod rose to the occasion, as always when in a tight corner.

'We are going to have a little go of skating before dinner' she answered airily. 'Come on, Jed. Help me to put my pattens on.'

But I couldn't take my eyes off Oamy. It seemed as if he held my eyes with his own, and I felt that he could see right through me, at the wicked thing we were doing, skating on Sunday, and at the lie we were acting out on Mam and Dad and everybody else who loved us. He pulled himself up so straight that he looked even taller than usual, and came on to the path at the top of the bank. When he spoke, his voice sounded deeper, and richer, and sterner than I'd ever heard it before. It was like Sir John, and the minister, and the doctor and the schoolmaster all rolled up into one.

'Jed' he said. 'Go home at once, and take Tod with you.' It never occurred to me to disobey a voice like that, and I turned towards Tod, expecting her to feel the same. But there was a red patch on each of Tod's cheeks and her chin was stuck out so you could nearly have tripped over it. When she looked like that, wild 'osses wouldn't turn her, as our Mam often said. She didn't speak. She just shook her head, to tell me she wasn't going home.

Oamy spoke direct to her, then. 'Tod', he said. 'I heard your father tell you last night that you were not to go skating today. Has he given you permission, in spite of what he said? If he has, give me your word that you are speaking the truth, and I shall not interfere. Does he know?' The colour had flooded all over Tod's face, but she wouldn't answer. I shook my head, miserably. Floss and Sar'anne were ready now, and down onto the ice.

'Come on Tod, hurry up' one of them called. 'Don't take no notice o' that mucky ol' tramp! It ain't nothing to do with 'im!'

Tod continued to screw one of the skates to her boot. She looked her defiance at Oamy, and made it quite clear she was going to follow the twins' advice, though I knew very well she couldn't get her pattens on properly without my help. I stood miserably between her and the tramp, when Oamy moved. He took two strides towards Tod, and lifting her foot in one hand, deftly unscrewed the skate with the other. Then he put both hands under her armpits, and lifted her up as if she was a doll, setting her down on the bank, facing home.

'Now go!' he ordered, motioning to me to go first. I shall walk behind you, every step of the way, till I see you safe home.'

Tod bowed to the inevitable. She never cried in a situation like this. She marched off with her head in the air, while I picked up her pattens and followed her. Oamy gathered his bundle up, and caught us up in a few strides, keeping behind us like a watch dog. Down on the ice, Floss and Sar'anne had reached the middle of the drain and were standing there holding each other up, while they called out insults to the tramp, and worse insults at Tod and me for being baby-cakes and taking any notice of him. Then, seeing that we didn't attempt to escape him, they struck out towards the mill, with their hair flying behind them.

We walked home in utter silence, Oamy about ten yards behind us. Tod's lips started to quiver at the thought of what Dad would say when he knew. But before we got to the planks, Oamy caught up with us. 'If you can put your skates back without being seen' he said 'you may rely on my word that I shall not give you away.'

Tod turned and looked at him, with her eyes full of tears. I knew she wanted to say she was sorry, but she couldn't.

'My word!' said Oamy. 'What good is the word of a tramp? But I give it, all the same.'

'Promise' said Tod.

'I promise' he answered.

Tod licked her finger and held it up. 'See this wet, see this dry' she began. But Oamy shook his head.

'See Tod' he said, fingering his bundle 'I'll swear an oath, like any gentleman. We haven't got a bible here, so I'll swear it on the most precious thing I have.'

He took out his little box, and held it in his hand. 'I swear on the silver new nothing. There, will that do?' Tod nodded, and I mumbled a thank you, somehow. Then we held our skates behind us, in case Mam should be looking out of the window, and left him.

We crossed the planks sedately, as if we were just coming home from chapel. We looked back at Oamy standing like a dragon in the path, in case we turned back, and we knew that he'd stay there till he saw Dad coming, which could only be a matter of a few minutes. Then we crept into the shed and hung our skates up again before we went through to where Mam was mixing a batter pudding on the table and Aunt Lizzie and Grammam still enjoying each other's company. We took our top coats off, and hung them up, ready for afternoon Sunday school. Nobody took the least notice of us, and though we didn't feel very good, we felt safe enough that our naughtiness would be overlooked this time.

Dad had been home about half an hour, and we had finished our dinner, when the Shallcross's big brother came to the shed door to ask if Floss and Sar'anne were playing with us, 'cos their dinner was ready. 'They ain't here' Dad replied, going to the shed door. 'Jed' he called. 'Have you seen Floss and Sar'anne this morning?'

It was Tod who answered, willing now to risk being found out if she had to be. 'They went skating, on the Catchwater' she answered.

Dad began to put on his coat, and reach for his pattens.

'Come on, George' he said. 'Go and get your father. We'll go different ways till we find 'em. They might have gone any one way.'

It was another half hour before Dad came back. He came in and said to Mam 'Shall you go round to Mis' Shallcross, and see if you can do anything?'

Mam looked in horror at him, a question in her face. 'Both on 'em' Dad said. 'In Old Rouncer's dipping hole.'

Aunt Lizzie got up from the table. 'I'll go' she said, seeing Mam look at us, and then sit down with her face like the ashes on the grate.

'Ah' Dad said 'I reckon as you'll be better at that job than Mam.'

Nobody spoke. They didn't want to talk about it in front of us. They didn't send us to chapel in the afternoon, but pushed us into the front room to 'play by ourselves' while they cleared up, as they said. There was nothing to play with, being a Sunday, though there was a fire there on account of Aunt Lizzie and Grammam being visitors. Tod and me never looked at each other, let alone spoke. The time seemed everlasting. I stood against the window shoving my hands down into my trouser pockets till my braces stretched as far as they'd go, and then letting them up again. Tod sat on the rug in front of the fire, staring at it. After what seemed about an hour, we each got a book and pretended to read, though the Bible I opened at the Psalms didn't help me at all, and when Tod turned the pages of *The Life of Christ*, she hurried past any page with a picture of an angel on it, so she didn't really read at all. We were stunned, and horrified and guilty, and I knew very well that neither of us would feel any better, ever, till we had told Dad all that had happened that morning, and our part in it.

There were two doors between the front room and the house-place, and a little porch between them where the stairs went up. We could hear voices faintly through the doors, and understood that Mam and Grammam were giving way to tears. Then we heard the back door open, and guessed that Aunt Lizzie had come back.

Tod looked at me, and I at her, for the first time in nearly two hours. She tiptoed across the room, and opened the sitting room door. I followed, and we went into the little porch, where we could hear distinctly through the other door.

Aunt Lizzie was sobbing out her tale. 'Both together on the big bed, side by side' she said. 'I hope as long as I live I shall never see another sight like it. And their hair, still wet, spread out all round their little dead faces, like a couple of angels.'

It was only then that Tod started to cry.

HELPING DOBSON

MY DAD WAS the only person I ever knew who actually sat at the very corner of a table to eat his meals. Most people sit at the side, or at the end of any table that doesn't happen to be round; but Dad never did. He would pull up his old high-backed Windsor armchair to the corner of the big mahogany table that stood in the middle of the 'house-place', and of course the leg of the table got in his way. So he could never sit as close to the table, either, as most folks do, especially as he always sat with his legs crossed, right over left. Once upon a time, when he was young, he had broken his right leg jumping off a cart, and it hadn't been set very well. So when he crossed his legs, the right foot dangled at a very queer angle. At the table it curled round towards Mam where she sat at the end, and swung about in a way that drew attention all the time to the fact that our Dad wasn't quite like ordinary men in a lot of ways.

This was made very clear to us all at meal times, but especially to Mam. Whatever she put on his plate he would eat with complete indifference, not because he didn't like good food but because he almost always had something a lot more important or interesting to think about than his grub. Mam said he simply wasn't worth bothering to cook for, and was always grumbling at him for 'golloping' his food; but he'd only laugh and say, 'Quick to eat, quick to work', and take no further notice of her. Altogether he irritated Mam at meal times in a way she never got used to, and it was as if his swinging foot, turned almost the wrong way round, acted as the last straw to her. She would keep looking at it and opening her mouth to speak and then changing her mind. Then us children knew by the way her eyes flashed and the strength of the bangs and clatters she made with the dishes that she was going to burst out with something before the meal was over.

Dad was 'golloping' a huge plateful of delicious, pink home-cured ham one Saturday tea-time when Mam suddenly exploded.

'That's my best ham you're eating, not cow-cake!' she said. 'You might at least take time enough to chew it to make sure it ain't brown paper and string!'

Dad turned his head towards her and paused with a bit of ham on the end of his fork. He looked sort of bewildered, as if he didn't quite recollect where he was, and as Tod said afterwards, he seemed as surprised to see Mam sitting in her place at the end of the table pouring his tea out of a big enamel pot as he might have done if she'd suddenly turned into a giraffe-necked woman from the Congo. I thought he was probably worrying about the war that had just started.

'Seems a decent enough sort o' chap' he said, opening his mouth and pushing in the ham. 'Very well eddicated an' all, I reckon.'

'Who?' said Mam, not at all sure whether to laugh at his queer ways (which she really liked) or to box his ears, or to cry with frustration because he still hadn't commented on her splendid ham.

'Who? Why – him as I'm talking about. Harriet's lodger.'

'Harriet's lodger?' Mam repeated, and her voice rose to a sort of squeak with astonishment. Her expression was so bewildered that they both now looked as if they were only elevenpence-ha'penny in the shilling, and me and Tod began to laugh.

'Are you telling me that Harriet's got a *lodger*?' Mam asked unbelievingly, setting down the teapot with a thump. 'Whoever in the name of thunder would want to lodge over there?'

That's what had been puzzling me, too. Our Aunt Harriet and Uncle John lived a good way from us, right in the middle of a huge stretch of fen that had never been drained properly. So it was a real wilderness of a place, and dangerous as well to anybody as didn't know their way about it. Some time in the past somebody had cut three long, wide canals (we called them dykes) right across it, and though they were never cleaned out now like other dykes they were still full of water about five feet deep all winter and in summer they dried up to thick, black oozy mud. You couldn't see 'em for the coarse grass and reeds and things that had grown up round them, and if you once stumbled into one of them in winter the chances were pretty high that the Hooky Man (who as all fen children know, lives in all the dykes and drains) would get you and pull you down.

Dad used to tell a tale about a bullock that got out from a farm and lost itself over there. Everybody in the district went out to help look for it, and just as somebody sighted it, it blundered into one of these 'cuts'. The man who'd found it ran as fast as he could to get some others and to tell them to bring ropes and poles, but by the time they got back to where it was, the poor thing had sunk in the mud so that only its nose was sticking out, and they couldn't save it. It just went on sinking till it had gone clean out of sight.

Between the cuts, and all round them, was the damp, marshy fen, as wild and desolate a place as you could ever im-agine. Here and there were bare patches where the old turf diggers had cleared the top growth of bushes and reeds off and dug out the blocks of peat to sell for fuel, and stacks of these turf blocks still stood where they had been left to dry. But turf-digging was getting to be a thing of the past now and the coarse grass had grown up quickly and covered the old turf-pits, making the ground dangerously uneven as well as boggy. This wild place was cut off from our fen by a wide drain, and down the side of the drain opposite to us there was a row of thick, tall black-poplar trees that it was a job to see through, even in winter. There was an old rickety tarred wooden bridge over the drain at one place, so you could get into and out of the turf fen if you had to, but not many folks ever wanted to. Us local people had no call to go over there, and strangers never came to the fen at all if they could help it. There was nothing for them to see there and nothing for them to do; besides, the whole district, even our well-drained farming land sometimes, was full of mosquitoes and snakes – particularly adders – that 'foreigners' didn't care a lot for.

The mosquitoes bit strangers all over. So they did us, but when we felt 'em bite we'd knock 'em off and think no more about it. Strangers couldn't treat them so lightly, because whenever they were bitten a great red bump would rise up in no time, and the next day there would be a big watery place like a blister, very itchy and terribly sore. Sometimes these bites made people really very ill, so that they talked wild, and sweated and shivered. But mostly the only effect was the nasty blistery places on any uncovered bit of skin the mosquitoes could get at. Folks used to wonder why they never bit real fen folks. Of course, as Dad explained to us, they did bite us all the time, but our blood had got used to them and so we didn't notice. Down by the drain, and over in the turf fen, they hung about in clouds, and attacked anybody silly enough to go there.

We went two or three times a year to tea with Aunt Harriet, though so far we'd never been allowed to go by ourselves because of the Hooky Man. We loved going over there in summer though, because the fen was a mass of wild flowers – forget-me-nots and yellow irises, toadflax and jonquils, cat's tails and feathery rushes; and down in the drain and the cuts we'd look for flowering rush, that we called 'hen and chickens', yellow water-lilies and arrowhead. Then there were a lot of butterflies that you didn't see anywhere else, and at night huge moths that Dad said were very rare, and bred over in the fen because they were undisturbed there. Of course there were all sorts of birds as well, and we always tried to find a last year's nest of a reed warbler, so that we could cut the three reeds it was attached to and take it home to put in the bamboo flower-holder that hung in the corner of our front room.

Anyway, our Aunt Harriet and Uncle John lived over there, right in the middle of the wilderness. Somebody a very long time ago had found a dry, solid patch close to the old turf diggers' track that crossed the fen from side to side if you knew where to look for it, and had built a place to live in there. There were really two cottages, end to end, with separate doors. Each of them had only two rooms, a house-place with a big open hearth, and a bedroom. When Aunt Harriet, who was Dad's oldest sister and donkey's years older than Dad, had married Uncle John, he had been earning his living by turf-digging, and they went to live in one of the cottages to be close to his work.

It wasn't too bad then, because Uncle John's sister Martha and her husband Timmy lived next door in the other cottage, and there were four young folks together to share whatever happened. Timmy and Martha soon had a lot of children, and couldn't manage to bring 'em all up in the little house, so they left; but Aunt Harriet and Uncle John never had any children, and they stopped where they were. By the time turf-digging was finished they'd been there so long they didn't want to move. They'd cultivated a little bit of ground that supplied most of their food, and Uncle John could always get work roding dykes out or thatching, or doing other odd jobs for farmers, because he was a very handy sort of man. Aunt Harriet had taken over the cottage next door a bit at a time so she now had a spare bedroom and a 'front' room, though you had to go out one door along the brick doorway and in the other door, to get to it.

Now it seemed she'd got a lodger to live in her spare room. We were flabbergasted, all of us. It seemed that Dad had been over there in the morning of the day I'm telling you about, to see if Uncle John would give him a hand with the harvest, and had heard the news and even seen the lodger.

'What's he like?' asked Tod, who was always first with the questions we both wanted to have answered.

Dad was a good talker, and enjoyed having a tale to tell.

'Well – he's tall, and big with it – about thirty I should think. He's sort of pink and white, if you know what I mean, with a skin like a girl's more than a man's and a lot of fair hair and a big moustache. His hands are as big and as thick as mine are, but they're as soft as a baby's bottom, and his finger nails are so clean I can't think he's ever done a day's work in all his life. He were just coming out o' Harriet's front room door when I got to the other door, so I bid him good day. He answered pleasant enough, though a bit short, and I could tell he were an educated fellow by the way he talked. Not from these parts, either.

Of course, when I got in to Harriet's I said "Who's that fella that's just come out o' next door?" and she told me how he'd come knocking at the door about a week ago and offered her a pound a week for her rooms for the rest o' the summer. A pound a week! It's more than poor old John's ever earned in all his life, I'll be bound. Harriet said he'd brought a lot of food with him, and said if he wanted anything else special he'd see about getting it. But she said he'd seemed very satisfied so far with pork and ham and fowl and Harriet's puddings and cake. She always was a good cook, and can make a meal out o' nearly nothing better than most folks, I reckon.'

Mam glared at him, being a bit offended at him praising his sister's cooking like that; but he was still thinking about the strange business of the lodger, and her glare was as much wasted on him as her beautiful home-cured ham.

'I suppose Harriet has to "do" for him – his washing and all that?' she asked.

Dad nodded. 'He has three meals a day and she does his washing' he said. 'But she don't have to make his bed or clean his rooms. It appears he's very fussy about his belongings and don't want 'em touched. So he asked her for a key and he cleans the rooms himself, and locks the door every time he goes in or out.'

'But whatever does he *do* all day?' asked Mam, voicing a question that I'd already been wondering about myself. She went on, sort of thinking out loud, and we could see she'd forgotten about Dad's foot and the ham. 'I have heard that folks as write books sometimes take and live in outlandish places till they get 'em finished, so as nobody disturbs 'em. That's what he's doing, I'll be bound.'

Having made up her mind, Mam turned her attention back to Dad's lack of table manners, but he was still deep in thought about the lodger.

'It's a queer thing for a young, strong, eddicated man to be a-wasting his time on in wartime,' he said. 'Ought to be ashamed of himself, anyway, if that *is* what he's a-doing over there. But Harriet said different. He ain't the only stranger there's been about there lately, not by a long chalk. It appears that the government think now that this war's going to last a lot longer than anybody expected it to. The Germans are going to try to starve us out – well, we know that a'ready. Anyway, Harriet says one o' the folks as 'as been over in the turf fen told her that somebody had had an idea of digging turf and mixing it with some stuff as gets throwed out when they're making sugar and using it to feed cows on. Of all the daft ideas!'

'Oh', said Mam, a bit disappointed that her theory about the lodger being a writer had been so quickly and so easily demolished. 'I suppose Harriet's lodger is one o' them gover'ment men, then?'

'No', Dad answered. 'That's what's so funny, to my mind. He aint nothing to do with 'em. Harriet said he told her it was on account o' them 'e was there, but not to do with 'em. It seems he's what they call a naturalist, only interested in flowers and birds and butterflies, and such. He says that if the gover'ment do carry out their idea it'll ruin all the wild life over in the fen. So, being so keen on it, he's come to find out all he can about it afore it's too late, and to make collections and records of everything what grows or breeds over there. That's why Harriet hasn't got to go into his room, ever. He says it'll be full o' jars and cases and boxes that he keeps his specimens in – bugs and beetles and fish and snakes and everything else. He particularly said as he intended to catch live adders if he could, and he wouldn't want Harriet to run any risks.'

'Well, I'll be sugared!' exclaimed Mam. 'Whatever does he want with adders, alive or dead! If I were Harriet, it 'ud be a long while afore I bothered to go into a room full o' snakes and beetles, whatever he paid me. Fancy though – a pound a week and no cleaning!'

She looked real wistful, envying Aunt Harriet such easy money, so that it made us all laugh.

'You'll p'raps get your chance an' all,' Dad said. 'I heard another bit o' news while I were out this morning. John told me that one o' the gover'ment men told him that they are going to turn Biggin Fields into a place for flying machines to land on – an aerodrome, I reckon they call it. John says there'll soon be hundreds o' men up there, working on getting it ready. No doubt some o' them will want lodgings.'

Tod and I had finished our tea, but Dad's second bit of news held us on our chairs as if we'd been glued there. Biggin Fields was about the only bit of grassy land for miles and miles all round us. It lay between us and our nearest shopping town, and now and again Mam sent us there to get her live yeast for breadmaking. It was five miles each way round by the high road, and she wouldn't have expected us to go if we hand't had our bikes; but there was a short cut through Biggin Fields, and in summertime we loved to walk to Ramsey that way.

Ramsey had been built hundreds of years ago on a bit of land that stuck up high and dry above the fens all round it, and Biggin Fields, though still flat, was on the edge of this high bit. Only high land was under grass round our way. The fens that had been drained were used for crops, every inch of them, though most farms, like our grandmother's, had one or two little grassfields for a few cows and the horses to graze. Now here was Dad telling us that Biggin Fields was going to be turned into an aerodrome! We had heard of course about the flying machines we were using in the war against the Germans, and Dad knew somebody who had actually seen one once; but we were soon going to have them flying right over us and settling on land that joined our own grandmother's fields. It simply couldn't be true!

When we finally left the table Tod and I went out and sat in our special place in the garden to talk it over. Our place was down under the old cider-apple tree. Nobody ever bothered to gather these apples, because they were too sharp for most people's taste, and didn't ripen till very late. We ate them all the time when they were ripe, though it was too early for that yet. But we regarded the tree and its corner as our property. One of us sat on the lowest branch, and the other in an old turf barrow we'd brought there for that purpose.

The thought of the aeroplanes was uppermost in my mind and I wanted Tod to talk to me about that; but Tod, who was always a lot cleverer than me, said we had to talk about Aunt Harriet's lodger. When I protested she said that the aeroplanes weren't here yet and the lodger was, and that by the time the aeroplanes came he'd be gone, so we'd better make the most of him while we could. One thing was certain – we had more claim on the stranger than any of the other children in the place, because after all he did live with our aunt and uncle. That made him our property, and we felt we had to know a bit more about him as soon as possible so we could boast about him at school on Monday morning. Meanwhile there was Sunday School next day. Would any of the others have heard about him? We decided that we should have to ask Dad a lot more questions at breakfast time, counting on Mam's own curiosity about him to help us.

Sunday morning breakfast was the only one of the week Dad had with us. He'd finish his yard work by about half-past seven, and come back home and wash, shave and change. Then we all had a cooked breakfast together – bacon and sausages, all home-made, before Dad and Tod and me went off to chapel, while Mam stopped at home to cook a beautiful Sunday lunch. We were waiting our opportunity to introduce the topic of the lodger when Dad suddenly took the wind out of our sails by suddenly saying to Mam; 'I said we'd be there by about four o'clock.'

'Where?' the three of us said, all together as if somebody had pulled a string to make us work.

'Where? Over to Harriet's to tea.'

'You are the aggravatingest man as ever any poor woman ever had to live with, I do believe' said Mam. 'You might a' told me yesterday and give me a bit o' time to get ready!'

'Why do you want to doll yourself up to go to see Harriet?' said Dad. 'I just forgot, talking about the aerodrome.'

We could see Mam was really very pleased, and so were we. We worked it out quick that it would mean we shouldn't have to go to either afternoon or evening chapel for one thing, and for another it was a glorious hot sunny day – just the sort of day to go for the long walk over into the fen. We loved Uncle John, though we were a bit scared of Aunt Harriet when she got talking about the Bible to us sometimes. But Dad protected us from her preaching as much as he could, and it was never very long before she and Mam started going over all the news of the neighbourhood, and then we were free to do as we liked.

We hardly knew how to get through the morning at Sunday school, and rushed home so fast Dad could hardly keep up with us. Then, after lunch, away we went. Half a mile down the drove, then over the old ricketty bridge, and we were in the turf-fen. We started to pick flowers, and reeds to make boats and whistles. We gathered cuckoo-spit off the rushes until Mam made us stop because it stickied our clothes, and we peeled thin rushes to get at the pith to make 'roses' and baskets with; and all the time we walked nearer and nearer to our first sight of the lodger.

Suddenly there was Aunt Harriet's tiny bungalow, standing low and long with its pink bricks and tiled roof, and blue peat smoke coming out of the chimney although the day was stifling hot, because that was the only way Aunt Harriet had of boiling the kettle for our tea. There was no sign of HIM anywhere, but Tod and I knew better than to show too much interest. The grown-ups would soon do it for us. The little house-place was crowded when we all got into it, and Tod and I were squeezed together facing the tiny window at tea time. So we could see through the window and the grown-ups could see through the door, which stood wide open of course, as it always did except in mid winter, to let the smoke out.

Suddenly Uncle John said; 'Ah! There 'e is, bor' – poking me with the knife he happened to be holding to draw my attention to the window. Everybody craned their necks to get a view, and we all saw him for the first time. He was about two hundred yards away, standing absolutely still, with grass and rushes coming up nearly to his knees. Every now and then he raised a pair of field glasses up to his eyes and then wrote on a little pad he took out of his pocket.

'What's he doing?' asked Dad.

'Same as he 's a-doing all the while, as far as I kin see,' said Uncle John. 'Helpin' Dobson.'

Now we all knew what 'helping Dobson' meant. It meant pretending to be busy doing something but not really doing anything at all. Anybody helping Dobson was being idle and not getting on with what there was for the busy folks to do. There was a lot of real scorn in Uncle John's voice, and I could sense straight away that whatever Aunt Harriet thought of her lodger, Uncle John hadn't much opinion of him.

'Has he catched anything yet?' Dad asked, still watching the distant figure.

'Not as I've seen,' said John. 'But he's got to find 'em first, afore he can catch 'em aint he?'

'He aint got to go far to do that,' said Dad. 'From what I could see as we come across the fen, if he stands still long enough they'll all come an' ask to be took. As for flowers and grasses and things, the children gathered enough on the way here to keep him busy for a week, classifying 'em and drawing 'em. That's what naturalists do, aint it?'

'Naturalists be jiggered,' said Uncle John scornfully. 'It's my belief he's come 'ere just to get out o' the way so as 'e don't have to go to the war. If 'e stopped in London or wherever he come from all the gals 'ould soon be giving him white feathers! But they do say as how the government'll soon have to call all young men up to fight, whether they volunteer or not. Then such as *him* (Uncle John jerked his head towards the stranger, both hands being busy with his tea) will have to go, like it or not. That's why he's come to a place like this 'ere. He thinks they won't find him here.'

'Hold your silly tongue, John Oliver, do!' said Aunt Harriet, exploding at last. 'You've got no call at all to take the chap's character away like that! For all any of us know, he's doing exactly what he says he's come to do. How's a hignorant country bumpkin like you come to know what a heducated gentleman like him's a-doing? You keep a still tongue in your 'ead and be civil to him, and I'll do the rest. As long as he dubs up his pound a week every Friday he can help Dobson till the cows come home, for all I care! So you jest mind what you're a-saying, in case he leaves us and gets lodgings somewhere else!'

'Ah, I'll tell 'im, when he brings the barrow back,' said Uncle John, and then everybody looked at him, because we knew by that answer that he'd said what he had said partly to tease Aunt Harriet, and had intended to make her fly at him. His old eyes were twinkling like little stars when he looked at Tod and he dropped one eyelid in a huge wink at her as he nodded his head to draw her attention to Aunt Harriet. She'd stood up and gone red in the face and her chest was pushed out like a pigeon's. She sank down in her chair again as if she'd been punctured as the men and us children chuckled, and even Mam, who had put on her most genteel manner with her best frock to come out to tea, giggled at the look on Aunt Harriet's face.

'You'll be the death of me, you silly old fool!' Aunt Harriet said to Uncle John. 'I ought to know you by now! I've put up with you for nigh on thirty year, an' you can still fool me!'

After tea we sat out in the sun on the doorway. Being Sunday, Tod and I weren't allowed any toys. But it didn't matter today. We were content to sit still and listen while the grown-ups talked about the war and the local boys who had volunteered (one had been killed, and Mam and Aunt Harriet cried about him), and the aerodrome and the government's idea for using the peat in the fen, and the lodger of course.

'What's his name?' Dad asked. Aunt Harriet and Uncle John answered together, each eager to be first; but whereas Aunt Harriet said 'Mister Misseldine', Uncle John said 'Muster Mussledine', and Tod giggled. The women in our family were forever picking us up in our speech and trying to make us pretend we hadn't got a fen way of talking, so Aunt was being genteel and saying the grand name as well as she could, but Uncle was turning it into his own language.

Tod had what Dad called 'an ear' for the way folks talked, and could mimic anybody so well that if you couldn't see her you'd swear it was the other person talking.

She was saying 'Mister Misseldine' in Aunt Harriet's Sunday-best voice and 'Mus' Musseldine' in Uncle John's alternately for my benefit, when the owner of the name appeared suddenly round the corner of the house. Everybody stopped talking, and we all stared at him. He was just as Dad had described him, only bigger and better-looking, and I'd never seen anybody wearing such beautiful clothes – well, not close to, at any rate.

'Ah, Mrs. Oliver! I see you have visitors. Don't let me disturb you' he said, and his voice sent shivers up and down Tod's spine she said, because it was so deep and educated. We could understand everything he said of course, but there was hardly a word come out of his mouth that sounded the same as it did when Dad or Uncle John said it.

While they went on talking I felt hot and uncomfortable,

and I knew for the very first time why Mam didn't want Tod and me to grow up talking like people did in our fen. She said everybody would know us for fen-tigers as soon as we opened our mouths, and we were going to know how to 'speak proper' if she had to leather us every day of our lives to make us mind her. As she very rarely laid even a finger on us, we weren't actually afraid of her strap, though we were always scared of her temper; but until I heard Mr. Misseldine standing there in the sunshine talking easily to all the grown-ups I'd never really understood what she was on about.

Aunt Harriet told him who we all were, and he shook hands with Dad and bowed to Mam. She was a very, very handsome young woman, our Mam was, and I saw that too for the first time as I caught the admiring look the lodger gave her and watched the pink flush rise up her long slender throat and cover her creamy skin right up to the roots of her lovely jet black hair, because she understood his look, too.

'Tod,' he said. 'Jed. What unusual names – but easy to remember, and I sha'n't forget them.'

There was a pause.

'Did you want anything sir?' asked Uncle John.

'Well – nothing that cannot wait,' he replied. 'I have just been looking for any visible sign of the pathway that Mr. Oliver calls 'the old caus'y', and wondering about it, but I see no trace of it anywhere. Can you tell me anything about it?'

He looked at Uncle John for an answer, but Uncle was making signs to Dad to be the spokesman. Dad told him how he reckoned it was the remains of a road made hundreds and hundreds of years ago, before the Romans come to this country, even. Whoever had made it, to help them get across the fen, they'd done a good job, because it was still there, buried deep under about two feet of peat that had growed on top of it since then.

'So you can't walk *on* it now, sir,' Dad went on; 'but all the same, if you cross the fen from here towards Sawtry Roughs way you'll most likely be walking along it. It went from the high place we call Honey Hill across to Castle Hill for certain, and I reckon that's how the rest of it continued, from high place to high place by the driest and safest route. I've dug through it many a time when I've been digging turf. Of course, there ain't much real danger walking over the fen now, because the peat is so thick. As long as you don't get into any o' the cut dykes you'll be all right.'

'Thank you very much,' said Mr. Misseldine. 'As it happens, I was going to ask about that, because I see from the map that there is a railway line quite close, and rare specimens can often be found in cuttings and on embankments. In such a wild spot as this that line may turn out to be a naturalist's paradise.'

'Yes,' said Dad. 'That's the main London line from the north. It's about two mile away as the crow flies.'

'You wont come to no 'arm in our old fen, sir,' Uncle John added, 'but if you should 'appen to fall in a cut, fling yourself back'ards against the side and grab 'old o' the grass w'yer 'ands. Don't mortar about we' yer feet in the mud, 'cos that'll on'y get you in wuss an' make yer sink faster. Pull yerself up on yer arms till you can find a solid bit to stand on.'

It was a long speech for Uncle John, and the gentleman thanked him gravely. 'I'll remember,' he said. 'I think I'll go for a little stroll now.'

He raised his hat to Aunt Harriet and bowed again to Mam, and strode off, with us all watching him. When he was about fifty yards away, he stopped, took out a pipe and tobacco and placidly filled his pipe. Then he put it in his mouth and, lighting a match, puffed and puffed till the blue smoke rose round his head.

'Sensible chap,' said Dad, laughing. ''E's evidently found out a'ready what our mosquitos can do to forriners.'

'Ah,' said Aunt Harriet. 'He were in a rare pickle a day or two ago, with bites on his face and neck. I had to give him my sody-carbonate to dress 'em with. And John told him if he smoked he'd keep 'em off a bit.'

The pipe took several matches to get it going well, but at last he seemed satisfied, and tossed the match away, still alight. Dad and Uncle John both sat up in their chairs so as to be able to watch better. Mr. Misseldine strolled on, but at the place where the match fell a little blue spiral of smoke began to rise and the crackling of yellow flames showed above the dry grass where a black patch appeared and started to grow. Then Dad and John were on their feet, scraping back their chairs on the old brick doorway.

'Numbskull!' said Dad unbelievingly. Then he started issuing orders. 'Mam! Harriet! – get brooms or anything you can, quick. Jed – pick up Aunt Harriet's rag rug – Tod'll help you. Quick John' – as Uncle John came back from the shed at the back of the house with a couple of spades. We all did as we were told, and rushed towards the fire, which was now speading fast.

'Round the edges, all of you – beat it out!'

We were wondering whatever we had to do with Aunt Harriet's best pegged rug, when Dad showed us, laying it over the flames and jumping on it. 'Keep at it!' he said, flailing away with the flat of his spade.

He suddenly looked up, and saw the lodger standing watching us in amazement.

'Come back and help, can't you?' Dad called, and the man did. Within a couple of minutes the fire was out. Mam and Aunt Harriet were a bit flushed and smutty, and Aunt was looking a little ruefully at her rug.

'It aint a bit hurt, Harriet,' Mam said. 'Not even scorched.'

'Ah, well, at least it's had a good shaking,' Aunt Harriet replied, and they went in again to lay the rug back in its place in front of the huge open hearth.

Dad and Uncle John and me and Tod were gathering up the other tools, and I could see Dad keep looking at the stranger as if he was trying to make up his mind to say something. It was the other who spoke first, however.

'I am very much at fault,' he said. 'It is unforgivable, in the beautiful countryside, to be so careless. I might have burned down Mr. Oliver's home, and my own precious equipment and belongings in it.'

When Dad spoke, his voice was so different from his ordinary one, sort of hard and cold, that I felt as if I'd fallen through the ice in the pond.

'You might have burnt the whole fen,' he said.

Mr. Misseldine looked uncomfortable. 'Yes – I did not realise how quickly the dried grass would help a fire spread,' he said. 'Indeed, I might have caused some of the very flowers and creatures I wish to preserve, to perish,' he said. ('Perish!' said Tod under her breath. She was obviously enjoying his queer talk.)

Dad looked at him, full in the face and fair and square. 'So you might,' he said, 'and that might ha' bin a bad do for you, bein' a naturalist; but me and John here, we don't care nothing much for a few wild flowers and things as'll grow again anyway, provided there's something for 'em to grow in. What I meant is that you could ha' set the whole fen afire – Don't you see, sir? I mean the earth itself. This 'ere fen peat is just dried grass and stuff, rotted down. It's ten feet deep in some places over here, and if it once gets afire there ain't nothing as'll put it out. A spark from a train set a fen afire the other side o' the line two year ago, and it's still smouldering now. Nobody knows how far it'll spread afore it's burnt its way out.'

He paused, then shouldered his spade. 'It's a pity the gover'ment don't tell you chaps from London a few simple facts like that afore they let you loose,' he said, and marched off, with Uncle John following him. Me and Tod lingered a bit, and we both noticed that Dad's words had had a real effect on the lodger. He went so white that Tod said she thought he was going to be sick, and I said that Uncle John was probably right. He was a real coward, in spite of being so big and strong, and Dad had frightened him to death.

When we got back to the house Mam was getting ready to

go home. Dad and Uncle John stood together on the door-way, still looking to where Mr. Misseldine was now sitting down in the grass.

'Well, that fair caps my behind,' Uncle John said. 'Fancy a heddicated chap from London not knowing that there!'

'Fancy a *naturalist* not knowing about the place he's come to better than that!' said Dad grimly. 'And fancy a *naturalist* throwing a match down, wherever he happened to be.'

He seemed real upset about it, and we walked home almost in silence. Mam was tired and excited, Tod and me were nearly too worn out to talk, though Tod kept treating me to the lodger's voice every now and the, saying 'All the things I wish to preserve, to perish!', and she made it sound so silly that I got a fit of the giggles and laughed all the last mile.

Even that didn't rouse Dad to take any notice of us, or play with us like he usually did when we were on a long walk home. He seemed sunk in thought of a serious kind, and it wasn't until he opened our own gate that he uttered one of his queer remarks.

'Ah well,' he said, 'there's more ways o' killing the cat than choking it wi' butter. Them as lives longest 'll see most.'

After a couple of weeks both the lodger and the aerodrome had had their time as nine-day wonders to talk about and Tod and me were looking forward to the long harvest holidays from school. We broke up on the Friday and spent Saturday and Sunday feeling free, but by Monday we had already begun to be bored. The excitement of harvest on the farm hadn't started yet and we were soon finding the days without school to fill up the middle of them a bit too long for us. On Tuesday Dad came in for his dockey in the middle of the morning and made a startling suggestion.

'Why don't you go and spend a few days with Aunt Harriet and Uncle John, over in the turf fen?' he said.

Mam was clearly surprised, but not put out. 'She's got nowhere to sleep 'em now the lodger's there', she said.

'No,' Dad replied. 'I've been thinking about that. They'd have to come home every night and go back in the morning. But they know the way, and Jed's old enough to take care o' Tod now. They've got to learn, anyway, to look after themselves. They know better than to go anywhere near the dykes and drains, and if they see an adder to let it alone. I see John this morning an' told him they'd go tomorrow. Harriet will be pleased. She loves having them about.'

As Tod said afterwards, it didn't occur to Dad to ask us if we wanted to go. We did, as it happened, partly because we felt grown-up to be allowed to go by ourselves, partly to give ourselves a change of occupation (until we got bored with that too), and partly because of the lodger.

Mam raised only one slight objection. 'What'll they do over there all day?' she said.

Dad laughed. 'Help Mr. Misseldine to help Dobson, I daresay,' he said. That was Tod's idea too. She took her penny exercise book from Woolworths and a brand new pencil with her. I'd filled mine with drawings of what I thought an aeroplane looked like, so I couldn't; but I had a secret hope that Uncle John would teach me how to catch adders alive in the same way as he could, so I asked Dad if I could borrow his old silk neckhandkerchief that he kept wrapped round his fiddle. I didn't expect him to say yes, but he was thinking of something else at the time, obviously, and nodded. I didn't ask again. I just took the beautiful old silk handkerchief, dark blue with gold-coloured patterns in it, and stuffed it into my pocket.

We went off early, and got to Aunt Harriet's place safe and sound by the time Uncle John came in for his dockey at half-past ten. We had Aunt Harriet to ourselves for a little while, and after we'd answered her usual questions about being good and saying our prayers and minding our books, we began asking her questions about the lodger.

'Jest the same as he were a fortnight ago,' she said. 'Still helping Dobson, all day and every day. Don't seem right, somehow – but who am I to question what a gentleman like him does with his time?'

'Have you seen the stuff in his room?' I asked.

She shook her head. 'It's as much as my pound a week's worth,' she said. 'I daresn't even look in the window. He's drawed the curtain so as I can't, anyway. Says the sunlight'll ruin his instruments or something. You can take his tea to him if you like tonight. We have to knock on the door an' he comes an' opens it a crack an' takes the food in. You can't never see nothing.'

He had, it seemed, taken his packed lunch with him out into the fen that day. We spent a pleasant time with Uncle John, and went back to the house at tea-time for a meal before walking home again. We saw the lodger when he came in just before tea-time, and Aunt Harriet boiled some water for him to wash with.

'Seems he washes all over every day,' she confided.

'I don't know what for, I'm sure, seein' as he don't do nothing to get hisself mucky. But he says he's used to a bathroom and can hardly bear to be without it. John has to empty the closet every day to please him – he uses the one belonging to next door all to hisself, so don't you go there! You use ourn, there's good child'en.'

The lavatories in question were round the back of the house, little huts in the garden; just a wooden seat with a hole cut in it over a big earth pit. Usually, they were only emptied about once a year, but Aunt Harriet said Mr. Misseldine had insisted that Uncle John fixed up a bucket under the hole and emptied it every day before half-filling it again with carbolic disinfectant – 'garribolic' Aunt Harriet called it, but we knew what she meant. 'Sich wayses!' she said scornfully.

We said nothing, because we knew that our Mam had been on at Dad to fix us up with a bathroom and what she called a 'chemical lav' for so long that he'd at last promised to do it this year if the harvest was a good one.

At tea-time we took the lodger's tea. He opened the door

about a foot but stood in the gap so that we couldn't see anything, though Tod said she thought she saw some white stuff on the wall behind the table.

'That'd be his towel,' I said. 'Aunt says he has to have a clean one every day!'

He came out on the doorway after tea and talked to us a bit. Tod asked if he'd managed to catch a lot of things yet, and he said no, he'd been busy with the grasses and flowers first, but he had seen the rare orange butterfly and was hoping to get some specimens of that before the week was out. We'd seen the orange often, but even we knew that it was not very common, and we quite understood why he wanted to get one.

'Have you got an adder yet?' I said, fingering the silk scarf in my pocket. He shook his head. 'They are shy of human beings,' he said. 'But when I am ready I shall look for them too.'

Dad seemed very interested in all we told him when we got home. We went again next day. Tod wanted to help the lodger catch an orange butterfly. I daren't tell anybody I wanted to catch an adder, because if they do bite you they can kill you, and I knew everybody would stop me from trying. My plan was to persuade Uncle John to find one for me, and then I'd whip out my handkerchief and hope that excitement would do the rest.

It happened even better than I have ever hoped. In the afternoon, Uncle John was coming home across the fen from where he'd been working. I don't know what he'd actually been doing, but he had his old turfman's heart-shaped hodding spade over his shoulder, with its broad blade glinting bright as silver in the sunshine. Mr. Misseldine was with him, and we rushed out to meet them both when they were still four or five hundred yards away from the house. While we were talking, Uncle took his spade down and leaned on it, and Tod as usual began hunting about in the grass for wild flowers. She suddenly sprang back and yelled 'Uncle John!

71

Here's a snake!' We all dashed to see it, and were in time to watch it wriggling away – there was no mistaking the tell-tale V-marks of the adder all down its back.

'Quick!' I said. 'It's an adder! Let's get it for Mr. Misseldine.' We began to look for it again – Uncle John, Tod and me.

'Keep your eyes open, and don't tread on it,' said Uncle John. 'Move slow, an' if you see him, keep behind him.' He turned towards the naturalist. 'You know of course, sir,' he said, 'as all adders are deaf. They can't hear you if they don't see you. We allus reckon that the adders say;

> 'If I could 'ear as well as see
> No man would be the death o' me.'

We fanned out, still looking. 'Here he is!' I said, and Uncle leaped toward where I was. We fell back to watch. John popped the bright blade of his spade down in front of the creature, which immediately turned and began to wriggle away in a different direction. Uncle nipped up his spade and blocked its path again. Time after time the adder turned, wriggled, darted off, twisted – but always the silver spade was there in front of it. The room it had to turn in grew smaller and smaller as Uncle's quick movements hemmed it in. Then, suddenly, it reared its head and struck at the spade. The poisonous venom sprayed out over the silver-bright surface, and began to run down the blade, turning it before our eyes to a most wonderful, vivid, deep purple colour, and staining the spade as if it had been sprayed with paint. Tod and I were fascinated, because we had often heard about turfmen playing this trick with adders but had never seen it done before.

Mr. Misseldine was standing almost too far away to see, but when it struck he said; 'Kill it! Kill it! Quick, before it bites the child!'

Uncle John was still keeping the poor thing penned in with his spade.

'I thought you wanted it *alive*, sir,' he said. 'Now if only I

72

had a silk neckhandkercher!'

I felt in my pocket and whipped out the one of Dad's I had borrowed for just this purpose. Uncle snatched it out of my hand and, throwing down the spade, began to tease the adder with the handkerchief instead, flipping the blue silk in front of the adder's eyes and snatching it away again as soon as the snake tried to strike. More and more of the big silk square was used with each flip, until suddenly the whole handkerchief was spread out before the snake just as it struck, stretched out in both John's hands to make a good target.

The adder struck again, right at the middle of the silk, and this time it wasn't withdrawn. The fangs went through the silk, and at the same moment Uncle lifted the handkerchief. There, high above the ground, was the captive adder, his fangs firmly tangled in the fine threads of the silk. We knew he could never get them out, and that Uncle John could now kill him with a blow the moment he wanted to. The snake hung wriggling from the handkerchief as Uncle turned towards the lodger.

'Ere 'e is, sir, alive and kicking as they say. You'll be able to get him off the silk and into a jar wi' a pair o' tweezers, I dessay. I'm seen other folks as are interested in sich things do it arter we'd caught the adders for 'em. Why – where's he off to?'

Mr. Misseldine was running as fast as he could toward the house.

'Gone to get his things, I should think' said Uncle John. 'There were no call for him to be in such a hurry. We can take the adder back to him.'

We waited a long time, and when he didn't return we set off ourselves towards home. I begged to be allowed to carry the adder, and Uncle let me. I carried the silk square at arm's length, watching the wriggling creature all the time, just in case he managed to escape, though I really knew he couldn't. When we got up to the house the lodger was nowhere to be seen, but Aunt Harriet was, 'on the rampage' as Uncle John said, because the pudding for tea was done and we were late.

'What in the name o' thunder were you up to?' she asked. 'I see Mr. Misseldine come flying 'ome as if Old Nick were after him, and he went straight to the closet and shut hisself up there. I went out to the back door, an' heard him reaching fit to throw his heart up. When he come out I went an' called at his door to ask him if he were ready for his tea, an' he said no, he didn't want nothing only to be let alone. He said his dinner ha'n't agreed with him, an' he was a-going straight to bed. So if the puddin's sp'iled, an' gone hard, it aint my fault or his'n. It's yourn, for being so late home.'

Then she saw the adder. 'Throw that thing down, Jed, an' come an' get your tea,' she ordered. Uncle John came and took the handkerchief. He split a willow stick and put the silk in the slit and then stuck the other end of the stick in the soft earth just beyond the doorway. So we went in and had our tea and left the adder still wriggling on the silk outside the lodger's door. It was still there when Tod and me went home, and I was a bit worried about Dad's handkerchief, but Uncle John said he'd keep an eye on it for me.

Dad was very, very interested in what Tod told him, though he seemed a bit put out that I'd taken the handkerchief from round his fiddle without asking him. When I said I had asked him and he'd nodded, he laughed and said he'd heard a nod was as good as a wink to a blind horse. He was always saying things like that – well, come to think of it, so was everybody else in the fen, an' all. Only Dad said things he made up for himself very often, as well as all the old sayings; and a lot of poetry and stuff out of books as well, because he was always reading, anything and everything he could get hold of. Mam said if he were on his way to be hung and a bit o' printed paper blew across his feet he'd stop the execution party while he read it. What he said now was:

'God moves in a mysterious way
His wonders to perform.

74

He plants his footsteps in the deep
and rides upon the storm.'

Then he got up and went out on our own doorway, just standing and staring across the fields. We soon forgot him and got ready for bed, though Mam said, for the tenth time just lately, that she wished she knew what was on his mind.

She wouldn't let us go to Aunt Harriet's the next day, or the one after, because it had started to rain and didn't seem to know when to stop. But the sun came out again on the third day, and away we went. Aunt had washed Dad's handkerchief and gave it back to me. I asked what had happened to the adder.

'It died,' she said, 'afore Mr. Misseldine felt better enough to deal with it. So John throwed it away, and I washed the handkercher so as it should be ready again when he wants another adder.'

Mr. Misseldine was all smiles and talk when we saw him, and apologised for having had to run away so fast. 'I think it was the apple pudding I'd had for my supper the night before,' he said. 'I am not used to eating fruit before it is quite ripe. London is very different from the country, you know.' We believed him.

Tod asked if we should go and try to find another adder for him.

'No,' he said, quite firmly. 'You see, Tod, I am a scientist, and scientists have to do everything in a careful, methodical way. I have been doing grasses and flowers, now I go on to butterflies and moths: after that to the beetles and bugs, then birds, and last of all the amphibians and reptiles.'

At dockey time Tod put on his voice and repeated it all, word for word, just as he'd said it. I told her she must be in love with him, but she said Dad had asked her to remember as many of the actual words the lodger said as she possibly could, so she could amuse him in the evenings when we got home. She liked 'amphibians and reptiles.'

After dockey time the lodger came and said he was going to try and catch an orange butterfly, and would we like to go with him. We were very pleased, especially when he brought out not one beautiful butterfly net but three, one each. Aunt Harriet said we could go as long as we didn't make ourselves a nuisance, but Mr. Misseldine said young legs were better than his middle-aged ones for such a job and he wouldn't have asked us if he hadn't wanted us. So off we went, and we had a wonderful time. We caught butterflies by the dozen, but not the rare orange one. Mr. Misseldine took a few and put them in his 'killing bottle' and let the others free again.

Just as we were all three beginning to feel hot, tired and thirsty for our tea, a bright orange appeared. We all went after it, but it seemed a specially clever butterfly. It drifted about, this way and that, but was never where we thought it was when we popped our nets down. At last the lodger said he was too weary and too hot to go any further, but Tod and me weren't going to give in like that. So he sat down, and we went on with the chase.

We'd forgotten altogether that we were running about the old turf fen by ourselves, and never gave a thought to anything but that butterfly. When it flew over one of the old boat-dykes we didn't hesitate to go after it, in spite of all the warnings about the Hooky Man. We chose a narrow place where the rushes and reeds and hassocks of grass were growing nearly into the middle of it, then stood well back, and ran and jumped. (We'd practised many a time, on little dykes, though we'd been forbidden to. Everybody in the fen jumped dykes to take short cuts, and you had to learn some time.)

We both got over safe and went on with the chase of the butterfly. We'd gone on a long way in front of Mr. Misseldine and had more or less forgotten him, when we suddenly heard a shout. We stopped to listen, and the butterfly escaped once more. It was him, shouting our names. 'Jed! Tod! Jed! Jed! Come back! Come to me!'

We looked, but we couldn't see him anywhere. 'He's playing hide-and-seek,' said Tod, and called out 'Coo-ee! Coo-ee!'

'Jed! Jed!' The shouts went on, louder and louder, and sounded queer, in a frightened sort of way. 'Jed! Quick! To me – come!'

We still stood there, the butterfly forgotten now.

'Where is he?' I said. Tod cupped her hands and called 'Coo-ee! Where are you?'

'I am here!' he yelled. 'Into the dyke I have fallen. Come to help me!'

'Isn't he funny!' said Tod. 'He's playing a game with us, and making up things for me to mimic. Come on, Jed – let's go and find him. We shall never catch the butterfly, anyway.'

We went back towards the place where we had jumped the boat-dyke – about the only place you could jump it, really, because the sides had caved in there at some time or other and made it narrow enough. We could see in a minute what had happened. The lodger had tried to jump it at a much wider place, to come after us, and hadn't managed it. He had landed on the other side, but not far enough over, and his feet had slipped down the bank and on to the bottom of the dyke.

It hadn't any water in it, after a long spell with only a couple of days of rain; but the rain had drained into the dyke and softened the hard, cracked crust the hot weather had formed over the mud. The lodger was a big man, and his weight had taken him straight through the crust and into the mud, up to his knees. As soon as he felt it sinking under him, he'd forgotten all Uncle John's advice and started to kick to free himself. That only churned up more and more mud, and made it soft, till he was in up to his thighs. Then he had grabbed the long grass and hung on, keeping still, while he shouted and shouted for help. We rushed along the bank till we stood above him. He was still shouting, with his face in the grass and his legs in the mud, gradually sinking lower. When he looked up and saw us he yelled again, in a frantic sort of way. We scrambled down the bank and tried to take hold of his hands, but he wouldn't let go the grass.

Then Tod took charge. 'We can't help him,' she said. He's too heavy.' 'Run, Jed, for Uncle John. I'll stop here. Be quick! He'll be all right as long as he keeps still.'

I went like the wind, across the dyke and all the way to Aunt Harriet's house. Luckily Uncle John was at home, and he didn't stop to ask questions. He snatched up a rope and Aunt Harriet's clothes prop and set out at a pace I would never have believed he could run. Tod was standing on the bank waving frantically, to show him where to come. Uncle ran to the side of the dyke, planted the prop like a vaulting pole and sailed over on to dry land with the ease of a man who'd done it all his life. I scrambled across at the narrow place and ran along the bank to them. By the time I got there Uncle John had laid the prop along the side and was looping the rope round the only bush near enough. He tied the ends of it to the prop and then lay down flat on his stomach to lower the prop as near to the lodger as he could get it.

The poor man was still yelling, in a frantic, despairing sort of way. 'Come!' he was saying, along with a lot of other gibberish. 'Come!' And once I thought he said something like 'Quick! Out of this get me.'

Uncle John told him to stop yelling and listen. 'Lay you still, sir,' he was saying 'and you'll be as right as ninepence. You aint in no real danger yet. Look up – and now when I say "Goo" do you let go the grass with one hand and grab the prop. I'll hold it, and keep hold o' the rope, so as you don't pull me in. Ready now – goo!' With a mighty effort of will, the lodger did as Uncle John said. Another effort, and both his hands were on the prop. Then Uncle John told us to pull on the rope till we could get hold of the prop, every time he said 'Heave!' So we did, and little by little we three and the bush that held the rope pulled the poor terrified man inch by inch out of the mud.

When at last he could get his foot on to the firm side our job was over. He climbed out, looked down at his clothes, and fell over in a dead faint. He came to after a minute or two, and we all had to get back over the narrow place. The lodger went straight to his own room, asking for water to wash with. We decided we didn't want to stop to Aunt Harriet's for tea. It had been upsetting in a queer sort of way, and we found we were suddenly terribly, terribly tired; but more than anything we wanted to be home, with Mam and Dad. Uncle John was a bit shook up, as well, and Aunt Harriet let us go without any fuss.

We told Mam our tale while she bathed us, and we were in our night clothes when Dad came in to hear it.

'Start again right at the beginning, and tell me every little thing just as it happened,' he said.

Tod, of course, did the talking. She had recovered quicker than me and was soon launched on her story, with all the cleverness of her mimicry to help her, waving her arms and legs about like an actress to make her points clear. When she reached the lodger's shouting she put on his voice so well that Mam and I laughed in spite of ourselves, and Dad looked up and said, 'Sh! It's no laughing matter, that it aint.' When Tod said, 'He kept yelling "Come! (only she said 'Com'): Quick com! Me out of this get!"' Dad stopped her, real sharp.

'Don't overdo it, Tod,' he said. 'You stick absolutely to the truth, do you hear! No putting bits on, now or any other time you tell the tale to anybody!'

'I'm not!' said Tod, nearly crying, because she hated Dad to be in the least cross with her. 'He did say that – just like I said!'

'Yes, I heard him,' I put in.

'Well, then, go on, Tod. What else?'

'Well, Jed ran for Uncle John, an' I stopped with Mr. Misseldine to show 'em where to come back to. He didn't take any notice of me, once Jed had gone, though I kept talking to him and telling him not to struggle more than he could help. But he kept yelling.'

'What did he say?' asked Dad.

Tod wrinkled her forehead. 'I couldn't understand him,'

she said, 'but it sounded like Got him, Himmel! Hill fur! Hill fur!'

Dad stood up, and his face was as white and strained as I have ever seen it.

'Go to bed now, both of you,' he said. 'We may have some pretty queer things to do tomorrow.'

In the morning, Dad asked us if we were rested enough to go back with him down to Aunt Harriet's. Tod said she didn't want to go, but Dad said one of us had to, so I went.

When we got there Dad marched straight into Aunt's house. She was sitting at the table with her apron over her face and crying.

'Harriet,' said Dad, 'Where's John? And where's the lodger?'

She took her head from under her apron and snuffled away her tears.

'Hello, Bill,' she said. 'John's gone to work as usual. He wont be home till late. Mr. Misseldine's gone up the caus'y for one more look along the railway line. He's just been in to tell me that after yesterday he don't want to do no more in the fen, so he's leaving tomorrow when he's packed his things up. An' I thought I was going to get his pound a week till the end of the summer!' She began to snuffle again.

'You'll manage without it,' said Dad. 'Now Harriet, you listen to me. Where's the key to his door?'

'Why, he's got it, to be sure,' said Aunt, bridling a bit.

'Come on, Harriet. This 'ere's a serious business,' said Dad. 'Don't tell me as you aint got two keys, 'cos I know better. And don't try and tell me as he's bin here a month and you aint sneaked in to see if he's keeping it reasonably clean. I know you.'

She still hesitated. 'Look 'ere, Harriet,' said Dad, real cross as I could see. 'If you don't give me that key straight away I shall break the door down. Now which is it to be?'

She went to the old black corner cupboard and took the key from behind a big cracked teapot that hung on a nail inside it.

Then we all went out one door and in at the other as soon as Dad had unlocked it.

Everything was extremely neat – the bed made, the towels folded, the papers on a little table stacked in neat piles. There wasn't a single flower, or grass, or insect or beetle to be seen; but the walls, as Tod had glimpsed, were covered with white paper.

'Maps!' said Dad. Just as I expected. He took his time, and examined each with care. 'The railway line, of course,' he said 'And the aerodrome. Then Ramsey, and all the whole district laid out as clear as if you were a bird looking down at it from the sky.' A strange look came over his face, and he swore, the first and last and only time I ever heard him do so. 'Struth!' he said, which for him was swearing, because he'd often told us it mean 'God's truth' and was breaking the third commandment. He kept on saying 'Struth!' and looking up into the sky as if he were seeing things up there over our heads. Then he stood up, put as all out, and locked the door again.

'I can't trust you, Harriet,' he said, 'so you'll come back home wi' Jed and me. You knowed all along as he weren't catching no specimens, nor sorting no grasses an' things. You just kep' quiet on account of that pound a week.' When she began to protest that it was nothing to do with him he shut her up quick and ordered her to get her hat and shawl.

We were soon back home, in spite of the time it took Aunt Harriet to puff her way up the long drove to the farm, where we lived then.

Dad washed, changed, and got his old bike out.

'I'm going to Ramsey,' he said to Mam. 'Don't let Harriet go home, if you have to tie her to her chair with a false-line. I don't want that lodger to know that we're on to his little game. I sha'n't be long.'

'Where's he gone?' we all asked; but we couldn't tell each other, and Tod and me soon went out to play. We wandered up the drove to the place where it met the high road.

We were still playing there when Tod looked up and saw a huge cloud of dust rising about half a mile away down the long straight road.

'It's a motor-car,' she said. 'Quick, Jed – let's put our ears down and listen to it!'

We always did this if by chance a motor-car did come down our road, which was about twice a year. We imagined we could hear the noise of it farther away if we put our ears to the ground, and perhaps we could. At any rate we could feel the vibrations it made as it bumped its way over the huge loose granite stones that the road was made up with.

When it got close we sat up to watch the wonderful machine go by. Even Tod was knocked speechless then. In the motor-car were two policemen – and Dad! We couldn't believe our eyes! The car came to the top of the drove, and then stopped. They couldn't get it any further than that, because it wouldn't go down the drove.

We got up and ran to where they were all getting out of the car.

'These are my two child'en, as I told you about,' said Dad. Then he turned to us. 'We're going across to the fen,' he said. 'You two stop here, and don't move till we get back. Watch the car and see that nobody else touches it. You can go home one at a time if you're hungry, to fetch some food, or some things to play with, but you don't both go at once. See?'

We saw. We didn't know what we saw, except that we'd been left in charge of a motor-car belonging to the police, and that we'd sell our privilege or leave our post by death's hand alone. 'Faithful unto death!' said Tod, standing by the side of the car like the Roman soldier in the picture that hung in 'the little infants' room' at school.

It was about three hours before anything else happened, and what did happen then was that another motor-car came up, this time with two very smart soldiers in it.

'Officers,' said Tod, in a whisper.

Soon afterwards, we saw the policemen and Dad coming

back up the drove. Only three went down, and there were four coming back. When they got near, we saw that the lodger was handcuffed between the two policemen. We shrank back to the side of the road when they got near, not liking to look, but not able to pull ourselves away. He was very pale, but held himself upright and proud. One policeman undid the handcuff on his side and the soldier stepped up and held his own wrist out for the bracelet to be put back on. The other soldier opened the door of his car. 'Get in!' he said curtly to the lodger. The three of them sat in the open back seat and the other officer climbed into the driving seat. It was then the lodger looked straight at us.

'Goodbye, Jed and Tod' he said. 'I shan't forget you. You did your best for me and we were friends.' And the soldier drove the car away.

Dad went back to Ramsey in the other car to fetch his bike back. We were all sitting round the table at home when he came in. He sat down at his usual corner, began to drink his tea, put it down again, and spoke to Harriet.

'Well, Harriet,' he said grimly, 'that's the end o' your lodger.'

'What's it all about?' said Mam. 'All I know is what the child'en told us, and I reckon they're making most of it up.'

Dad shook his head. 'He were a German spy, Harriet,' he said. 'You weren't to know that, so nobody'll blame you.'

'How did you find out?' she said. 'You don't *know*, either.'

'I had a good idea right from the first that there were something wrong about him,' he replied. 'So had John. Only we didn't tumble to it then as he was a spy. We just thought he wasn't what he said he was, a naturalist. A naturalist knows about the place the things he's looking for live in – no naturalist would have set the grass afire in the fen after a summer like we've had this year. Then again, no naturalist would have run away and been sick at the sight of a snake. Them as sent him just didn't know the sort o' place they were sending him to. I thought it funny as Harriet wasn't allowed to do his room out

– you *should* have reported them maps, Harriet, when you'd seen 'em. You'll have some explaining to do about that if the police ever find out.'

Harriet said, looking him straight in the eye, 'How did I know he wasn't doing 'em for our side?'

Dad knew when he was beaten.

It was Tod who asked the next question.

'Dad,' she said, 'what will they do with him?'

I could see Dad struggling, but with him, truth was truth.

'They'll most likely put him up against a wall and shoot him, my pretty,' he answered.

Then Tod put down her head and began to cry. So did Mam and Aunt Harriet. Dad looked stern and sad.

'Ah, that's how it is in wartime,' he said. 'That's what makes it all so wrong, to such as us. We don't know nothing about trade, and politics, and things as cause the wars atween countries, and as long as it's only countries you don't know nothing about fighting each other, it don't seem to matter much. But when it's the boys as you know yourself as go to the front and never come back, that's different. A spy's a spy. This one took his chance o' being found out and shot same as they all do. As long as it happens somewhere else, you don't think much about it; but when it's one as you know, who's been enj'ying Harriet's apple puddings right up till last night, that's different again. And it's us, a-sitting round this 'ere table, as give him up to be shot!'

Tod sobbed, and Aunt Harriet started to cry afresh.

'But there's other things to remember, an' all' Dad went on. 'If we'd a-let him get away, we shouldn't a' got off either. If you, Tod, hadn't told me exactly what he said when he fell in the cut-dyke, or if I hadn't told the police about them maps, do you know what would have happened? Afore long the captain o' some Zeppelin would a-bin using 'em to drop bombs on *us*, here, on grandmother's land, very likely, because it joins the new aerodrome. And on Harriet's and John's house, because it lays near the main line to London.

84

And if they'd hit the line with bombs and blowed it up, then thousands o' children in London might not have had anything to eat for days, and the soldiers and sailors no grub, and nothing to fight with. So you see, we had to hand him over – we didn't have no choice. If we feel bad about it, it's because war makes everybody bad.'

'He didn't seem like a bad man,' said Aunt Harriet mournfully.

'He wasn't a bad man, Harriet,' explained Dad patiently. 'He were a good *German*, as made a few mistakes. I reckon all spies have to be trained somewhere, and get a bit of experience easy-like, at first. No doubt them as sent him here had heard about us fen-folk having webbed feet and being a breed of numbskulls not able to tell a big A from a bull's foot. The worst mistake he made were to count too much on folks like me and John being the ignorant clodhoppers folks as don't know us take us to be.'

I was still having difficulty in taking it all in. 'Will they really shoot him dead, Dad?' I asked.

Dad nodded. I reckon for a minute he didn't trust himself to speak.

'Well, there's nothing else we can do for him, now,' he said at last. 'So the best thing as we can all do is to put him out o' mind, and forget as it ever happened, soon as ever we can.'

'There's one thing as we can do for him, this minute,' said Aunt Harriet, suddenly herself again. 'We can pray for him, same as we should for any man in trouble.'

She took our consent for granted, and we all stared down at our plates while she began to plead for her lodger with the only Authority she ever really knew about or understood, I reckon. Usually when she prayed aloud at the table she raised her voice and ordered God about a bit, but this time her old fenland voice was soft and pleading, and to tell you the truth I had a real job not to join Tod in her sobbing.

'Amen,' said Dad, when Aunt Harriet had finished. And we left it at that.

NINETY AND NINE

WE HATED SUNDAYS – though I hated them worse than Tod did. No toys, no games, not even books were allowed. We were scrubbed and cleaned and dressed in our best clothes to go to chapel for Sunday School in the morning and again to the service in the evening. Very often we had to go to afternoon service as well, because we were on the list to have the visiting preacher to tea, and that was worst of all.

After the evening service we walked home in groups, and that was good, because I could often be with my friends then; but our family nearly always stopped half way to call in at Dot's home, or else Dot and her parents came home with us. This didn't seem to me to be fair, because at such times Tod had Dot but I had nobody. When we called at Dot's home, Mam and 'Aunt Rose' would sit in the best room with Tod and Dot, talking, while Dad and 'Uncle George' would sit by the turf fire in the house-place telling each other tales. Neither lot of them really wanted me, and I used to have to hang about doing nothing till the time came for the hymn singing round the harmonium.

Aunt Rose and Uncle George could both play it (so could Tod by the time she was eight, and after that Dad bought us a piano). We stood or sat round in the front room and chose our favourite hymns. Dot always chose 'Only an armour-bearer, proudly I stand', and Tod usually went for 'There were ninety-and-nine that safely lay/In the shelter of the fold.' I liked 'Pull for the shore, sailor, pull for the shore.' The grown-ups specially the women nearly always chose mournful ones, it seemed to me, like 'Rock of Ages' or 'Jesu, lover of my soul' – though to do Dad and George justice, they'd usually ask for 'Diadem' at the end. 'Diadem' is the tune to

'All Hail the Power of Jesu's Name', and it's a jolly good tune that makes you want to sing.

We'd had a lovely hot summer that year, and the harvest was early. Dad worked for his mother, who was the farmer; but he had a bit of land of his own at the back of our house as well. In his 'spare' time he looked after and ran one of the many mills that pumped the water out of the dykes into the main drains, from the drains into the rivers and from the rivers into the sea. There wasn't much work for him at the mill in the summer, when he was needed most on the land; and when he was needed at the mill, in bad weather, he could be better spared from the farm. So it worked out alright that way, and he could do both jobs. He worked nearly every hour of daylight, summer and winter, and often all night at the mill as well. In the ordinary way he would be gone from home by about half-past-five in the morning, riding his ramshackle old bike up the muddy or dusty drove. In summer he'd be gone by five, especially in harvest time.

At that time of the year, as soon as Mam had done her housework and packed up food for us all, we set off and went after him, to spend lovely long summer days in the harvest field. We fetched and carried for the men at work, taking them cans of hot tea when they stopped for a break and running with their bottles of cold tea from the dykes (where they were put into the water to keep cool) when they wanted a drink as they worked. Mam and the other women made straw bands for the men to tie up the sheaves of corn with, after the reaper had cut it. Tod and I knew how to make bands well enough to give one of the women a rest now and then.

At dockey time we'd all sit round on a horsehoe of sheaves, or in front of a specially built, outsized stouk if there was any wind, and eat whatever Mam had packed up for us. Dad would climb down off the reaper, and hang the horses' nosebags over their mouths, and then come and fling himself down flat on his back with his cap over his eyes, and be asleep before Mam could get his bread and cheese or his ham sandwich out of the basket. He'd only have a catnap of about five minutes, but it seemed to freshen him up as much as if he'd had a good night's rest.

He'd been hard at work all one Saturday carting his own crop of wheat from the field behind our house and making a stack of the sheaves just behind our pigsties. He'd borrowed a horse and cart from the farm (he could only do that on Saturday afternoons) and he only had Tod and me to help him, but by the time the dew began to fall we'd got a lovely oval stack about eight feet high. We helped him to cover it with a big heavy stackcloth, and held the ropes while he tied it down to stakes so that the wind wouldn't lift it off if we had a storm. Then he put a ladder up the side of the stack so that Tod and I could go up and bounce about on top of the stackcloth. We loved to do that.

Next day it was our turn to have the preacher to tea, and Tod asked Mam if Dot could come back from afternoon chapel with us, and if we could have our tea out on top of the stack. Much to our surprise, Mam agreed. She made us some little sandwiches and gave us a pot of tea all to ourselves, and a slice of cake each. So we took it all up to the top of the stack to eat.

Then Tod said: 'I wish it wasn't Sunday, so we could have the dolls and the tea-set out.' I saw her eyes go sort of wide and round like saucers, and next instant she'd gone down the ladder like a snake. In a couple of minutes she was back, with her teaset in an old basket and her rag doll Betsy sitting on top of it.

'Coo! You'll cop it!' I said.

'Ssh! Don't you tell anybody, Jed, and they'll never know. I had Betsy and the teaset yesterday in the field, and Dad carried 'em up and left 'em in the copper house on top o' the pollard bin while he fed the pigs. He forgot to bring 'em into the house, and that's why they didn't get locked away last night.'

So we had a real doll's teaparty up on the stack, and though

I thought it was all very silly and a girls' game that I was a lot too big and too old for, it was a lot better than having to sit up to the table for Sunday tea with the preacher, and mind my manners all the while. In any case, Tod and Dot were so busy with the doll and the cups and things that I ate all the cake, and they didn't notice.

When Mam called us to come down and get ready for chapel she stood at the back door and waited for us, so we were in a real mizzy-mozzy to know what to do with the teaset and Betsy, because we daren't let Mam or the preacher see we'd been playing with them on 'the Lord's Day.'

'Leave 'em up here,' Tod ordered in a whisper. 'I'll come up and get them in the morning.' So we went down, and left them there.

Dot's mother and father came all the way home with us that particular Sunday night, to have supper and taste the first of the hams Mam had cured in the spring. She always cooked one in harvest time, so as to have plenty to cut at when Dad was at work so hard. She'd cooked her very best one (in the copper) the day before and it was *huge* – weighing about twenty pounds, as near as I can guess now. When she cut it, it was all juicy pink inside, and the sight and the smell of it made your mouth water.

'You'll have to take your mother a bit in the morning,' Mam said to Dad. 'She does give me credit for being able to cure a ham to suit her, if nothing else.' (She didn't hit it off very well with Grandmother, mostly.)

'Ah, I will,' Dad said. Then Mam went on: 'And I'll go round by the road in the morning an' take poor old Mother an' Father a mossel or two as well.'

'Ah,' said Dad again. 'I hope Grammam'll be well enough to eat a bit, poor old gal. It'll do her good. And it aint as if we can't spare it, for I never did see a bigger an' better ham. We shall have our work cut out to get through it while it's good.'

Well, everything went on as usual till the Thursday night of that week. The weather had got hotter and hotter, and everybody was beginning to get touchy with the heat and with tiredness.

When Dad came in and began unlacing his shoes, ready for his supper, Mam was setting the table. She looked real cross and sulky, and suddenly she said 'Did you take your mother half a score of eggs this morning? You might have asked me first. I'd been saving them brown eggs special.'

Dad was drawing his chair up to the table, and for once he didn't look his usual cheerful self. His hair was standing up on end and his face was still streaked with sweat, though he had washed his hands. He wouldn't have his proper wash till he went to bed, because he'd got his own yard-work to do after supper. He glared at Mam and said: 'I ain't touched no eggs! It ain't *my* mother as gets things for nothing from this place, I *can* tell you! If you're half a score of eggs short, they'll be at The Carriages I'll be bound, not up at the farm!' (Grammam lived in The Carriages, and Grandmother at the farm.)

Well, Mam was just coming out o' the pantry with the bread in her hand, and her eyes glinted and her hands shook, and we could see she was so savage and upset that she was going to cry at any minute. In the ordinary way that would have been enough to make Dad change his tune, and he would have made a joke and smoothed it all over. But not to-night.

Mam set the bread down in front of him with a thump, and beside it a lump of cheese, and a raw onion. Dad looked at it puzzled, as if he hated it, though usually he asked for nothing better.

'Where's the ham?' he asked. 'Hadn't I better have a bit o' that while it's still good? I had bread and cheese for my dockey at eleven o'clock, and we didn't stop for nothing only a drink at tea time. I'm been looking forward to a good plate o' that ham.'

Mam stumped into the pantry and fetched the ham out. She banged it on the table and began to cry.

'You've had your share of it a'ready, from what I can see!'

she said. 'I told you to take your mother some on Monday, but you needn't have took her all the best of it every morning o' the week. She's had all the meat, and now she can have all the fat and the bone. An' it's the last ham I'll ever take the trouble to cure, so now you know!'

Dad looked as near 'savage' as I ever remember him looking. He began eating the bread and cheese, pushing the ham away from him, and glaring first at it and then at Mam – really angry, it seemed. Tod and I kept very still. We were so upset we didn't want anything to eat, but in any case neither Mam nor Dad remembered to give us anything. We were used to Mam 'chuntering' at Dad, and we hated it, but we weren't used to them actually quarrelling, and we were frightened. We both understood quite well how Mam felt about our farmer grandmother. There was no love lost between them, as the saying is. Grandmother thought Mam was a pretty face and nothing else, because from the first she had refused to go out and work on the land as most other women did. Mam in turn thought Grandmother a hard old woman who was mean for the sake of being mean, because although she wasn't well off, she certainly wasn't poor, as Mam's parents were; but she didn't give much away.

'When Dad spoke again, his voice was growly with temper.

'You know as well as I do where the ham's gone,' he said. 'You know as I don't grudge your poor old mother anything as I'm got in the world, specially now she aint well. But it sticks in my gullet that I'm got to eat bread and cheese after working all day like I've been doing, while that good-for-nothing father o' yours sits in a pub eating my ham sandwiches.'

He pulled the ham towards him and glared at it again, and then shoved it across the table towards Mam as if it would bite him. She was crying harder than ever, and shoved it back without looking. But Tod and I looked, and we could understand what they were both talking about. The beautiful ham we'd started on only five days before was three parts gone. There was a knob of dried lean meat left at the knuckle end and a huge lump, nearly all fat, at the thick end. Between the two there was about eight inches of bare bone where all the best of the meat ought to have been.

Well, Mam and Dad went on shouting at each other, and pushing the ham about, and picking it up and putting it down. But by this time the quarrel had gone far beyond the ham, and when Tod began to cry, Mam turned and ordered us both up to bed. We looked to Dad for protection, but it didn't come. 'Yes, clear off to bed – now!' he said. Tod said 'We haven't had any supper,' but Mam raised her hand and said 'Did you hear me?' and we didn't wait for anything more. Tod cried herself to sleep, and I made plans to run away the next morning.

We'd been asleep for about three hours, I reckon, when we were both roused by an almighty clap of thunder that shook the house almost as if it had been struck. Now Mam was terrified of thunder, and so was I, though Dad and Tod simply didn't seem to bother about it at all. I scrambled out of my bed, frightened nearly to death, and went and pulled Tod out of hers, and together we tumbled into our parents' room. They weren't there.' Then we realised it was still not really dark, so we ran downstairs. And there they were, just where we had left them.

Looking back on it after all these years, I can see the funny side of it. They'd obviously been quarrelling right up to the minute of that terrible clap of thunder, but when that had happened, Mam had shrieked and flung herself at Dad to be taken care of, as she always did. And he'd jumped up and put his arms round her and pulled her down on his knee, as if she had been Tod. We'd seen it happen so often before that we knew exactly why it was we'd found them like that – only this time they were still glaring at each other like strange tomcats, and Mam had cried till you really could hardly see she had any eyes at all.

When they saw us standing there, they both looked silly and ashamed, and Mam was just going to get up when another terrific clap of thunder sent us all scuttling to Dad. Then Tod said, 'I *am* hungry,' and both of them looked guilty. Dad pushed us all away and began cutting Tod and me great doorstep sandwiches from the ham. He said to Mam: 'Well, as far as I can see, that cat must have had it. It must be the only cat for a good many miles around as can use a carving knife.' Then he lifted the knife, and said. 'Hark!' and we harked. It had begun to rain, so fast that the noise was nearly deafening, especially on the corrugated iron roof of the shed at the back of our house.

'It's a good job I've got most of the corn cut,' he said, in a more normal voice than we'd heard all the evening. 'This lot'll bash any that's still standing down flat in no time.'

The rain kept on, and at last we all went to bed, with a kind of sulky truce existing between Mam and Dad.

It went on raining – day after day, night after night. After the weeks of long sunny days we had weeks of long wet ones. The dykes filled, and Dad had to begin going to the mill at nights, pumping. The corn that hadn't been carted when the weather broke still stood in the stouks, sooden with rain, and what corn hadn't been cut at all lay flat on the ground, matted together. On one or two afternoons the August sun broke through the clouds, producing a steamy heat that was the very worst thing for the farmers, because it meant that the grains of wheat and oats and barley all began to sprout in the ear. Little white shoots grew out from the growing corn, and from the stouks, as if they'd all got suddenly old, and their hair had turned white overnight.

Dad spent more and more nights at the mill. As the days went by, the dykes and drains grew full till the water was level with the land and Dad and all the other pumping millers around had to stop with their mills day and night, to keep the water from overflowing the banks and flooding the fen. Dad got so short of sleep that he had to have a man to help him at the mill, so that he could snatch catnaps now and again. He'd come home most evenings so black he looked like a sweep, with his eyes all red and staring from lack of sleep, to have a wash and a meal before going back again for the night. He had to go to the farm twice every day as well to look after the horses, but apart from that there was little he could do there.

Then came a night when it rained faster than ever, and one of the banks of the main drain got carried away by the water, in spite of all the scradging the gangs of volunteers could do to build it up. Then water simply poured out of the gap in the bank, all over the fens; and when we got up in the morning it was as if we were living on an island in the middle of a swamp. Not all the land was under water, but a lot of it was, and out at the back of our house, a little way away, a field of our neighbour's corn that hadn't been carted stood up to the bands of the sheaves in the flood. In front of the house the land rose a little, and it was a bit drier that way. We could get out and on to the high road, as well as to the only shop, with care. Tod and I were glad that both Dot and Dickle lived on that side of us, because it meant that they could occasionally come and play, or we could go over to them. After the night when the bank blowed, the rain stopped, and the sun made a few watery appearances. Our neighbour borrowed the little boat Dad kept down at the mill, and Dad helped him to fetch his harvest in, a few sheaves at a time, by boat, bringing it back to stack on a high place, in case any of it should be any good when it had dried out.

Dickle and I watched them rowing out to fetch it, across the fields, and we thought it looked like good fun. We wanted to be outside all the time, once it stopped raining, after being cooped up so long inside. But though we were allowed to play in our yard and round the hovels, we were absolutely forbidden to go away. The reason, Dad explained, was that while the fields were so covered with water you couldn't really tell where the dykes and drains were. So though you wouldn't be likely to get drowned in the flood waters themselves, you might step by mistake into a drain with sheer twelve foot sides, and then the Hooky Man wouldn't be long in getting you and pulling you down forever.

So we hung about the yard, splodging through the puddles, and getting very naughty and bad tempered. Grandad Rattles came one day to see Mam. He was an old scallywag, but I loved him and he loved me. On this day when he came he'd made me a catapult (a toy Dad had always forbidden), and Dickle and I played with it when Dad wasn't there, and hid it in the barn when he was. I remember I killed a sparrow with it, and Tod and Dot pretended it was a cockerel or a goose or something, and plucked it and cooked it with a tiny potato or two in one of Tod's dolls' saucepans. But they didn't eat it, because when it was cooked they remembered that they hadn't taken its innards out.

Well, there came a day when nobody was about but me and Dickle, because Tod had gone across the play with Dot, and Mam had gone to see Grammam, who lived on the high road. The water was beginning to drain off the droves a bit, though it was still deep all over the fen between us and the river. Dickle and I played with the catapult for a little while, but we soon got fed up. Then we talked about Dad and our neighbour fetching the corn in by boat, and looked to see if the boat was still there. It wasn't – which was a disappointment, for we both had the same idea of trying a journey in it on our own. After all, we both thought, we couldn't get drowned if we were in a boat. So we were thoroughly frustrated, and as full of mischief as two boys who have been bottled up for a long time can be.

We went into the copperhouse, where Dad boiled up potatoes for the pigs. By the side of the copper was a big wooden tub that was used to put the hot potatoes in when they were boiled, so that they could be mashed up with pollard from the bin and any scraps from the house for the pigs' supper. The tub was empty, though dirty. We tried to lift it, and found we could. Neither of us said a word to the other, but we both knew exactly what we were going to do. We took that old tub out and splashed across our field till we got to where the water was deep enough to float it, and then we climbed in. Dickle stepped in it, hanging on to a bunch of reeds, while I splashed back to find us a paddle of some sort. I took the old worn-out shovel that Dad kept in the copper-house to shovel the potatoes into the copper, and off I went back to the tub.

There was just enough water to float us, but we could feel the bottom here and there with the spade, and every now and then we got stuck on a bit of ground that was sticking out of the water. We couldn't steer our round boat, of course, so it simply took us more or less where it wanted to, and when at last we looked up, we found we'd travelled a fair way. What with carrying the tub right across our field through mud and water, and taking turns with the shovel to push us off when we got stuck, we'd worked jolly hard, and were beginning to get tired. But there was no way of getting home except by the way we'd come, so we thought we'd better start.

We'd got stuck on a particularly high and firm hump just as we made our decision to turn back. Dickle had been pushing and shoving with the spade on his side till he was red in the face and out of breath.

'Have a go on your side, Jed,' he said, handing me the shovel. So I stood up and plunged the shovel down with all my might to find the bottom and push us off – but the bottom wasn't there! The spade went straight down into the water – and I went after it, for the sudden movement had tipped the tub and me off balance. Before the cold water closed over my head I knew what had happened. The hump we'd been stuck on was the bank of the main drain, and I was in about ten feet of water. And I couldn't swim.

I won't tell you about the next minute or two. For one thing I can't really remember, and what I know about it is what Dickle told me afterwards. I struggled and thrashed about, and came up to the surface, but I'd got all my clothes on, and I soon went under again. There'd been too many children drowned in our fen for Dickle not to know all about it – in fact one of his own brothers had been drowned a year or two before. He was still in the tub, and was nearly frez with terror. He understood as well as I did what had happened, and as soon as he could collect his wits he scrambled out on his side, up to his waist in water, and came round the tub, holding on to it. By a lucky chance (for me) the shovel had floated back up to the side, close against the tub, and by leaning over, Dickle had managed to get hold of it before I came up to the surface for the second time. I was still struggling feebly, and fast losing consciousness; but Dickle still keeping hold of the tub, hung out as far as he could and with his other hand he pushed the shovel towards me. I clutched at it, and held on. So did Dickle, and little by little he dragged me towards him. I shall never know how he managed to get me up out of the drain and back into that tub, but the fact that I'm here now proves that he did. I must have fainted or something, I reckon, because I don't remember any of it till I came round again, sitting in the tub, and saw Dickle standing in the water against it, crying and shouting.

Good old Dickle! He'd saved my life. He's been dead a-many year now, and I often think about it, for he never did get a word of credit or praise for what he did, for the rest of his life. You see, we never told a soul what had happened. We knew we should get into enough trouble as it was, so we made a bargain, as soon as ever I could speak again, not to tell anybody. And we never did. This is the first time I've ever broke my promise to Dickle by letting anybody know what really happened that day.

Well, you'd think that being very nearly drowned would have been enough punishment for one day, but it seemed it wasn't. I soon came round, and I was sick, I remember, and was cold, and shivered so I couldn't keep still for a long time. Then I wanted to go to sleep, but Dickle kept at me to help him, because that tub was still stuck fast and we couldn't move it. We pushed and shoved and tugged – but we were too close to the drain to take any chances, and in the end Dickle got back in to the tub with me, nearly as wet as I was, and we realised we should have to stop where we were till somebody came to look for us.

When Mam got home in the dusk, having collected Tod on the way, and found I wasn't there, she didn't worry at all. She thought I'd gone home with Dickle, who lived quite close to the mill, and had then gone down to Dad at the mill and would be coming home with him. So it wasn't till he came home from work for his wash and his meal that anybody knew we were missing. Dickle's folks weren't bothered either, because they knew Dad would be going back to the mill later and expected he would see Dickle safe home on his way there.

When Dad had gone all round our buildings, shouting and getting more worried every minute, it was nearly dark. He lost no time in going over to get Dickle's father, and between them they called out all our men neighbours, with lanterns, to start a search. Of course, not one of them expected to find either of us alive. There was nowhere in a flooded fen we could be playing till it was dark, so of course they all believed that what they would find would only be two little dead, drowned bodies. And as it never occurred to any of them that we could possibly have gone out behind the house into the worst flooded part, they spent their time searching the dykes and drains on the higher side, in front.

After two or three hours, the helpers one by one began to give up hope and go home, till only our two poor frantic fathers were left searching. They went to the mill and got Dad's little boat and started off down the main drain with a lantern set up in the middle of the boat. Now Dickle and me, wet through and cold, hungry, tired and frightened to death, huddled together in the little tub and cried. And, strange as it may seem, we cried ourselves into a deep, deep sleep; so we didn't see the lanterns bobbing about across the fens. But all of a sudden I was roused into wakefulness by Dickle scrambling up to his knees.

I was awake in a moment, because I was terrified that he would tip the tub over and shoot us into the drain again; but he had started to shout, and then I got to my knees as well. Coming towards us was a glow in the darkness. We had heard a lot of old tales about Will-o'-the-wisps and Jack-o'-lanterns, and how they were the ghosts of folks as had been pulled down by the Hooky Man – and in all that dreadful night the moment that we first saw that light was probably the worst of all, for me at least. But the next minute we heard voices. Then we both tried to shout, but it seemed as if no sound would come, for what seemed like hours. Mine came at last, a hoarse croak that I should never have known was my own, when I recognised the shape of Dad's head silhouetted against the lantern that Dickle's father was holding up and peering at the water with.

'DAD!' I yelled. 'Dad! We're here!'

Well, it wasn't long before we were home, and in bed with hot bricks to our feet and flannel petticoats tied round our heads. They put Dickle in Tod's bed, and rubbed our chests with camphorated oil and goose-grease. They gave us a few drops of sweet spirits of nitre to make us sweat, and made us eat a great basinful of horrible onion gruel apiece to 'lay warm in our insides'. But they never grumbled – not a single word. And it wasn't until after we were fast asleep that Mam and Dickle's mother sat down and cried and cried and cried (Tod said), while Dad went off by himself to have a few words in private with 'the Lord' that he had such belief and faith in. There'd been many a prayer reaching the Lord that night, you may depend, and Dad was always one to show his gratitude.

Things were soon back to normal, of course. Neither me nor Dickle suffered anything worse than stiffness and tiredness, and that wore off after a day or two. The water began to go down, the sun came out, and the men began to work hard to save what they could of the crops and to clear up the damage the flood had done. It was about six weeks since the thunderstorm had broken the weather when Dad was able to leave the mill and start his ordinary pattern of work again, and it was then that Mam cooked her second best ham. She and Dad had quite forgotten their quarrel about the first one in the trouble of the flood and the fright of thinking I was drowned.

So it really was 'a capper', as Dad said, when on the second morning after the ham was cooked, Mam missed about a pound of the finest meat again. And on the third day she fetched it out to show Dad, and more had gone, as well as some eggs. They just did not know what to make of it, and things were very uneasy for all of us.

On the Wednesday night Dad was late home, and came in very tired after a long day. It was already dark, and Tod and I were ready for bed, but Mam had let us wait up till Dad got home. I was sitting at the table drawing cats and Tod was sitting on the hearthrug in front of the turf fire singing to her dolls. Dad sat down to supper at the corner of the table, and the ham, with a lot of bone showing, was on view once more. Neither Mam or Dad mentioned how fast it was disappearing, because neither of them wanted another row; but the sight of it made both of them quiet, not talking as they usually did. Tod had begun singing hymns, and had reached her favourite:

'There were ninety and nine that safely lay
In the shelter of the fold;
But one was far on the hills away
All out in the rain and cold.'

Her voice faltered, and all at once she began to wail.

'Oh! Oh!' she wailed. 'That's my poor old Betsy! That's my poor old Betsy!' And she began to cry as if her heart would break.

Dad picked her up and tried to comfort her. 'What about

your poor old Betsy, my pretty!' he said, and she sobbed; 'She's the one far on the hills away, all out in the rain and cold – on top of the stack!' And out tumbled the tale of how we had left Betsy out six weeks ago, so she had been there right through the flood.

'Fetch her in!' Tod kept saying. 'Poor Betsy! Fetch her in!'

Dad explained that he couldn't go and get her in the dark, and even if he did, she'd be so sodden wet that she couldn't be brought into the house. He comforted Tod by a solemn promise that the very next morning, before he went to work, he'd fetch Betsy down and hang her on the clothes line to dry. He kept his promise of course, and the stray lamb was soon back in the fold with the ninety and nine. But that wasn't the end of the story.

When Dad came in that night, he was very thoughtful, and over supper he said. 'Mam, I want you and Jed to get up tomorrow morning when I do.'

'*Whatever* for?' said Mam, bridling a bit, because she was afraid he was going to ask her to go out and help in the field.

He said: 'I can't be sure as I'm right. But I see something this morning that I don't like the look of at all. I got my bike out as usual to go to work, and I'd got a little way down the drove when I remembered I'd promised Tod to fetch Betsy in for her. So I throwed my bike down where I was and come back across the garden and jumped the dyke to get to the stack. And when I were coming down the ladder I see something move in the yard, and I could very near swear as it were somebody in our copper place.'

'Who?' asked Mam, unbelieving. 'Why didn't you go and see?'

'Well,' said Dad, 'whoever it were hadn't got no right there. And whatever could she want there – there's nothing worth taking.'

'She?' said Mam sharply. 'WHO?'

Dad looked uneasy. 'Old Nance White,' he said.

Now Nance was a poor old woman that lived with her

brother Joe that wasn't quite right in the head, in a little tumbledown cottage farther down our drove.

'I can't be sure, mind you,' said Dad, 'because I didn't see her, I only sort of caught a glimpse. And I was late already, and by the time I'd pegged Betsy on the line I couldn't waste any more time. But I've been thinking about it all day, on and off, and I want your help in the morning.'

So before he went to bed that night he made plans. First, he cleared the cupboard on Mam's side of the hearth of her sewing machine and all our toys, and put them out of sight in the front room. Then he sorted out a score of the very best brown eggs and left them on the pantry shelf in a colander, next to the ham – on which he left the carving knife, all ready.

At half past four next morning he called me out of bed. Mam was already dressed. I put my trousers and socks on and went downstairs. When it was nearly five, Dad sent Mam back upstairs, to stand against the little landing window, from where she could see into the yard. He told me to get into the toy cupboard and shut the door except for a tiny crack that I could see out of. Then he put his boots and his cap on, took his flagon basket on his back, and out he went as usual, to work.

Inside the cupboard I could hear my own heart beat, and smell the jam that was on the shelf above my head. It seemed like a year that I'd been there before I heard a noise at the door of the house-place that led into the shed at the back, and the next moment, through the crack in the cupboard door, I saw old Nance White come in. She had a coarse sacking apron on over her clothes, with a pocket in the front of it, and a man's cap on her head, while her arms were wrapped up in an old knitted shawl. She come in as bold as brass, and stood listening for a moment. Then she went to the cupboard on Dad's side of the hearth where he kept his things, and poked about on his desk that was on top of the cupboard. She moved across as if she was coming to my cupboard next, but stopped in front of the mantelpiece and took Tod's moneybox down. She went to the table and used a knife that was lying there to get the coins out – there was threepence-ha'penny in it. She put the money in an old purse and dropped it back into her apron pocket.

After that she went into the pantry. It seemed hours before she came out again, with a pile of slices of ham in one hand and five eggs held up against her chest with the other. She went to the door that led up to the stairs and listened, then laid her stolen goods down on the table while she made careful preparations to leave as quiet as she'd come. She took a bit of paper from Dad's cupboard top and folded the greasy ham up in it and tucked it down into the big apron pocket. Then she picked up the corners of her apron to make a little nest, and carefully placed the eggs in it. That left her with one hand free to open and close doors. She'd be gone in another minute – but just then I heard Mam coming down the stairs. So did she! She turned to go out of the door into 'the shed', but that was the moment I'd been waiting for. I put my head out of the cupboard and yelled: 'That's copped you, Mis' White! That's copped you!'

She turned to face me and sort of fell on the table, gasping for breath, just as Mam came through the stairs door. Mam was as white as a ghost and looked as if she was the one who had been caught stealing. I thought she was going to let Nance go, so I yelled: 'She's got some eggs in her apron and some ham in her pocket and Tod's money in her purse!'

Nance said: Oo! I aint, Missus! I aint, Missus! Oo, I aint, Missus! Oo, the little liar! I aint, Missus!'

Mam didn't know what to do, she was so timid, and just as I was getting desperate, because Nance had turned again to the back door, Dad appeared from nowhere, and blocked it. Then Mam sat down 'all of a heap' and began to cry, and I came out of the cupboard.

Dad said: 'You'd better get off back to bed. I'll deal with Nance now.'

106

When we came down again she'd gone, and Dad was calmly sitting having a second breakfast. He told us what had happened. He'd pretended to go to work as usual, taking his bike out of the shed and wheeling it to the gate, where he got on it and rode off. But he only went about a hundred yards up the drove, just as he had done on the morning he'd come back to get Betsy. He'd hid his bike in the dyke and slipped back across the garden to the lavatory, from where he could see the back of the house.

He'd realised that if anybody was stealing from our house it must be somebody who knew exactly what happened every morning. All the fen knew that he left for work about five and that Mam didn't get up till seven. (Nearly every other woman had to get up to get her husband's breakfast, but Mam wouldn't and didn't, and Dad never wanted her to, anyway. But there was a lot of talk, envious no doubt, from the other women about this, especially as it was one of the things Grandmother has always held against Mam.) Then, as Dad said, everybody knew Mam was deaf, so as soon as Dad had gone the coast was clear, because nobody ever locked a door. Why should they? Houses were a long way apart, and there were no strangers about.

Dad had worked it out in his mind that Nance had come across from her cottage before he was up, and had hid herself in the copperhouse. As soon as she'd seen him go, she could be into the house and help herself and out again without anybody being any the wiser. How long it had been going on would never be known. Things had been missed a good many times before, but neither Dad or Mam had said anything, because each thought the other was taking them to somewhere else.

'What are you going to do?' Mam asked. 'Are you going to the police?'

Dad shook his head. 'There's ninety and nine as safely lay,' he said. 'I reckon old Nance is the one, like Tod's poor old Betsy, left out in the rain. I warrant she'll be a long while

107

before she takes anything again after this morning, even if she has the chance.'

Mam bridled a bit. 'Are you going to let her get off like that?' she said.

Dad nodded. 'Well – not quite,' he said, ''cos I don't reckon that would be good for her. I've told her she's got to come and dig my potatoes in the garden when they're ready, to pay for what she's had. That won't hurt her. And I let her keep the ham and the eggs. She said they hadn't got a bite of anything in the house, 'cos neither of 'em's been to work while this flood's been out. So I told her to send Joe across in the evenings for a week or two to help me get the rest of the wheat in and to do the yardwork if I'm late home or at the mill. I hope he'll wash before he comes. The last time I see him I said: "Joe, your neck could do with a wash", because you could have sowed onion seeds in the muck in the creases. But all he said was: "I darsn't, maister. I darsn't. Every time I put water on the back o' my neck it makes my nose bleed."'

Even Mam laughed then, and Dad could see he'd done what he'd intended to do, which was to get the whole thing over and done with before he left. So he put his cap on again, ruffled my hair, kissed the top of Tod's head, and looked at Mam.

'You'd better think about getting another pig killed,' she said, skilfully avoiding any more direct reference to the ham.

'Ah. I'll tell him. When he brings the barrow back,' Dad replied, and away he went to work.

MILES' BOY

TOD WAS ALWAYS cleverer than I was. She was quick to understand anything, and then quick to make use of what she found out. She had usually asked a question and got the answer before I'd even worked out what it was I wanted to know. But I could do things with my hands a lot better than she could, because she had no patience at all, and Dad said that evened things up.

Dad was always trying to arrange things so that they were fair for everybody. When we were very little, Mam used to tell us the old rhyme about what little girls are made of. She would of course say

> 'Sugar and spice
> and all things nice'

and Tod would bounce up and down because she liked it so much. Then Mam would go on:

> 'What are little *boys* made of?
> Snips and snails
> And puppy dogs' tails.'

Then Tod would laugh and crow, and point her finger at me – and I would be expected to enjoy it all as much as she did (though I certainly didn't. I used to hate it).

One day Dad told us the rhyme instead of Mam. But he began with the bit about little boys being made of snips and snails and puppy dogs' tails. Then he said:

> 'What are little girls made of?
> What are little girls made of?'

and while Tod was waiting for her special verse he paused to think and then went on:

'Grass and twitch
And thistles and sich.'

Even Tod laughed, because she could see it was only fair, and Dad always made things sound funny anyway.

So mostly Tod and I got on very well together, but of course we both had other friends as well. I liked to do things with other boys, especially my friend Dickle (his real name was Richard George Albert). Tod often went to play silly girls' games with her best friend Dot. They always seemed to be playing dressing up games, especially one they called Kings and Queens. They had a little 'house' in the carthovel, and there they would set out bits and pieces of old china. In it they swaled around draped all over with long trails of convolvulus leaves and flowers, crowned with daisy chains and whatnot. Dickle and I used to make fun of them, and go off to our own concerns. But we very often found Dad sitting with them drinking a 'pretend' cup of tea and calling them 'Your Majesty', and such like.

This split between boys and girls nearly always happened towards the end of May, when the Chapel Anniversary came round again. Tod and Dot and the rest of the girls appeared to think and talk about nothing else for weeks before it actually took place. They used to get to the chapel for hymn practice hours before they needed to, and learned their 'pieces' (of poetry) so well that they could all say each other's as well as their own without a slip. They talked about what they should sing and who they should sing with if they didn't happen to be one of the stars chosen to sing solo, till us boys thought them all out of their minds. But worst of all was the way they whispered and giggled, and gave out broad hints, (without ever actually telling) about the most important thing of all to them – what they were going to wear for the great day. However poor families were, and whatever it cost the mother of the family in pinching and scraping and saving, as well as going out to work, everybody had to have something new to wear at 'the Anni', and by time-honoured custom the details of the new clothes had to be kept a deadly secret until the very afternoon they were put on for the first time.

Us boys approached the Anni with a very different set of feelings. For us, it cast a gloom over the summer from about Easter onwards, and we never felt free from it till the second Sunday in June was over and we could forget it for another year. It didn't worry us that the most we ever got in the way of new clothes was a new shirt or a new pair of boots that we should have had to have anyway. The ordeal would have been just as bad without them, and was no better because of them. We had to give up a lot of the precious light spring evenings to learning the special hymns and our pieces, and on the day itself our misery could hardly be told.

Us children sat on benches arranged each side of the pulpit, facing the congregation. The boys sat all together on one side and the girls on the other, while 'infants' of both sexes sat in the front row of both sides so that they could be quickly removed by their blushing mothers when they began to cry or wriggle or show signs of needing to be taken 'round the back.' On the girls' side, the organ was also mounted, with the organist, her back to the congregation, bouncing and 'sciencing about' among the new frocks – like a caterpillar wriggling in the heart of a cabbage, as Dad once said.

On the boys' side we sat there with our hair plastered down with water to make the unaccustomed parting stay put. We were all either squeezed into last year's suit now too tight for us, or conscious of the one that had been handed down from an older brother, being far too big. We clutched our special anniversary hymn sheets in hands that no amount of scrubbing with hard yellow soap would make clean, and we dreaded, with awful anticipation, the moment when the preacher announced 'Let us begin our day of worship by singing hymn number 444' (or whatever). Then we had to rise from our

113

benches in one concerted movement so as not to leave any-body sitting on the end of a bench and tipping it up, to the confusion of the whole arrangement. That moment was the worst of all for me.

It so happened that our Mam sat in the very front seat (facing the boys' side), because she was deaf, while Dad sat in the seat behind her, where he had always sat since he was a little boy himself. When we stood up to sing, they stood up as well; and that meant that my face was nearly level with theirs and only about three or four feet away. The effect on me was terrible. There was Mam looking me over to see if my nose was clean and my jacket buttoned properly, and I felt, rather than saw, the signs she made to me with her eyebrows or with her little finger cocked up, telling me to stand up straight, or take my hand out of my pocket.

Dad had the opposite effect on me – I couldn't help staring straight at him as if he was some strange creature I'd never set eyes on before. I used to see all sorts of things I'd never noticed about him in the ordinary way. How his hair stood up in a ridge all round the back of his head, for instance, where his workaday cap always rested, and how his right thumbnail, showing clearly against the red hymnbook, had a deep cleft down the middle of it; and how queer it was to be able to see the words of the hymn coming out of his mouth like bees out of a hive, instead of hearing them coming from behind me like I did on ordinary Sundays when Tod and me sat in the front seat with Mam.

Tod said she had this last feeling about Dad as well, but for her it was different. She said that when she saw him opening his mouth so that the words of the hymn could get out, especially the first hymn, which was always

> '*Praise* ye the Lord! 'Tis – good – to – raise
> *Your* heartsandvoices in – *His* – *Praise*'

it sort of took hold of her and lifted her up somewhere so high that all Mam's frownings and mouthings at her across the chapel couldn't get at her. In fact, Tod confided, it was all she could do to keep from giggling out loud when she looked at Mam all primped up and being so ladylike, with her mouth pursed up into a little button to sing. But Tod said she forgot Mam when the Anni really started, and stayed up there on a sort of hill of her own till the very last minute, when Dad's voice (among all the others) singing the last words of the last hymn –

'For grace and salvation
O *PRAISE-YE-THE-LORD!*' –

told her it was all over. Then, like everybody else in the congregation, Dad would sink down and bury his face in his hands to mumble a few words before giving the individual and hearty 'A-men' that turned him (and us) back into our ordinary selves again.

I really do not want to remember the ordeal of 'saying my piece' and the rest, so I sha'n't. I'll get on with my story instead.

All that I'm telling you about now happened when Tod and I were quite young. In fact, in this year of the Anni we all had such good cause to remember, I was only nine (nearly ten) and Tod was about eight and a half.

It began when I was roused from sleep very early that Sunday morning by little shrieks and squeals of delight coming through the wooden partition that separated my bedroom from Tod's. As soon as I was really awake I remembered what day it was, and my heart dropped nearly through my mattress with dread. My next thought was that Tod must really have taken leave of her senses, because although I knew she always enjoyed the Anni and all its goings on, it seemed to be carrying it a bit too far to be making such a hormpologe about it at six o'clock in the morning. The next instant, though, I heard Dad's voice coming from Tod's room.

'Careful!' he said. 'Hold him tight. I shall get in such a row with Mam if he makes a mess on your sheets.'

I scrambled out of bed and ran to Tod's room, and there she was, sitting up in bed cuddling a tiny wriggling, squeaking bundle of pink satin that turned itself, when I got near enough to see properly, into a newborn piglet. Dad held another in his long brown hands, and Tod leaned first over one and then over the other, kissing their wet wiggly little snouts. Well, what a thing to make such a fuss about, I thought indignantly. So I turned and was on my way back to bed to prepare as well as I could for the coming ordeal of saying my piece, when Tod asked, 'Dad, how do the sows get their little pigs?'

As usual, she had asked the very question I had wanted an answer to, because only in the previous week Dickle's brother Jacko had been teasing us about not knowing. 'You're too little to know about such things,' he'd said, and all the big boys in the school yard had gone away giggling and sniggering about it. So I stood rooted to the spot, waiting for Dad's answer.

'Well,' he said, 'they weren't there last night when I went to look at the old sow, but when I got up this morning there were ten of 'em.' (Actually, he said 'ten *on* 'em', but our teacher got ever so cross with us if we ever said that.)

'That doesn't tell me *how* she got them,' Tod persisted. 'Do tell me, Dad! I want to know.'

'Lawks,' said Dad hurriedly. 'There's Mam a-getting up! I mustn't let her see these up here.' And off he scuttled down the stairs as if he had a mad dog after him.

I went into Tod's room. 'I can't hear Mam getting up', I said listening.

Tod gave me a look of withering scorn. 'Silly!' she said. 'Of course you can't, 'cos she isn't. You know she never does get up on Sundays till eight o'clock, even when she's well. And she isn't well, because I heard her telling Mrs. Harper that Aunt Lizzie was coming today for the Anni and was going to stop and look after her while she stopped in bed. Dad just made that excuse because he didn't want to answer the question.'

That wasn't like Dad. We looked at each other, but neither of us had any explanation.

'They're all alike over some things, even Dad' said Tod. 'Grown ups, I mean. They'll go on for hours telling you about things you don't want to know, and grumble at you for asking questions when you really do. Look at Aunt Harriet and the Bible. She was going on like anything about the lilies of the field not spinning and weaving, the other day. When I said I couldn't see anything special about 'em *not* spinning and weaving, and that it would only be worth mentioning if somebody had found some actually doing it, she said I was a wicked girl as wouldn't go to heaven and she'd have to pray special for me that night for making fun o' the Lord's words.

Then she and Mam started whispering to each other about Polly Wilson's baby being born so soon after she got married. And I heard what they said, and asked what was wrong about that. Then Mam went red and Aunt Harriet looked as if she'd bit a crab-apple by mistake, and both of 'em told me to go away. But I wouldn't, and said I only wanted to know. And I said I wanted to know about Polly because I was sure she'd been married to Herbie quite as long as Mary had to Joseph when she had baby Jesus, 'cos Miss Cornell had told us about how they'd had to set off for Bethlehem as soon as they were married, and they'd only just got there when Jesus was born.

Then Mam got real savage an' slapped me – my arm – well, she would have done, only I dodged. An' Aunt Harriet shut her mouth together like a rat-trap, and started glaring at Mam as if *she'd* done something wrong. So I got up and ran outside. But I never got my answer. That's what I mean. They're all alike. Ask 'em any question about babies, and they'll go all silly and tell you to wipe your nose and wash your hands, or anything to get rid of you. I bet I find out, anyway, afore Aunt Harriet sees any lilies spinning and weaving. Though I like the bit about 'Solomon in all his glory'.

Tod was absolutely right, of course, and I nodded, and opened my mouth to agree with her. But she'd forgotten the beginning of the conversation, and was saying 'Solomon in all his glory' over and over again to herself.

Then I remembered it was the morning of the Anni, and I'd got to say my piece in public a few hours from now. So I asked Tod to hear me say it, and then I heard her say hers, till it was time to get up. When we went downstairs to breakfast we were very surprised to find our Grammam there. She said Dad had asked her to come and look after us because Mam wasn't going to get up, at any rate till it was time to get dressed for the Anni. So off we went to our last hymn practice, this time sitting on the prepared benches so that we could practise standing up all together and so on.

When we got home for lunch our Aunt Lizzie had come as well, and Grammam was still there. This was always a part of the Anni, like a midsummer Christmas. Families came together from a long way away. Mam hadn't got up though, and we really were surprised – and a bit put out too when we understood that she wasn't coming to the Anni at all. Aunt Lizzie got us ready, and inspected Dad to see if he was all right (he always left shaving lather behind his ears). It then turned out that Aunt Lizzie wasn't coming to chapel either, because she thought she ought to stop with Mam, and that Grammam was too tired and not very well.

Tod nearly cried, in spite of her new blue dress and her pretty white shoes and straw hat. But I was really worried, because I knew very well that Mam wouldn't have missed us saying our pieces for anything, so she really must be ill. Aunt Lizzie took us up to see her when we were all ready, and she looked perfectly all right as far as I could see. Tod asked her outright what was the matter, and she said her back was bad. She kissed us and told us to behave ourselves and say our pieces well, and off we went.

We children sat in our places whispering while the grown-ups who had brought us stood outside the chapel and talked till it was time for the service to begin. After the afternoon service we had to rush home to a quick tea and then go back

again as soon as we could for a 'run-through' of the pro-
gramme for the grand evening service, when the Minister
would be there and the chapel would be crowded, even to the
gallery. Tod and I half expected to see Mam with Grammam
and Aunt Lizzie in their places in the front seat as usual, but
when the preacher announced the hymn, Dad was there with
only a few strange children from the next village sitting in
front of him. If that wasn't remarkable enough, I remembered all my piece without a hitch, while Tod, looking
towards Mam's empty seat, stopped singing in the middle of
her duet with Gwen, who was so surprised that she stopped
singing as well, and they had to start the verse again. Tod was
scarlet with shame, and hardly looked up again for the rest of
the time.

But this queer day wasn't done with us yet. When we went
outside the chapel, where everybody stood about talking and
laughing and greeting people they hadn't seen since the year
before, Dad was waiting for us. With him were Dot's mother
and father, and my friend Dickle's mother. 'Ah,' said Dad,
'What do you think? Here's Aunt Rose asking if Tod can go
home with her to stop all night with Dot, and Mrs. Potts says
that isn't fair to Jed, so he'd better go and stop all night with
Dickle. I've said you can, because then Grammam can have
your bed, Tod.' And without waiting to see what we thought
about it he strode off towards home.

Tod looked for a minute as if she was going to cry, but she
changed her mind and rushed off to tell Dot, who'd wandered
off with some cousins from Ramsey that she didn't often see.
I was bewildered and embarrassed, because I'd never stopped
a night with Dickle's family before, and although I liked
Dickle a lot I detested his brother Jacko. But Dad had gone,
and I was left to deal with the situation as well as I could.

We soon started off towards the Potts' cottage, which was
in the opposite direction from our home. Dickle and I ran
along throwing sticky-burrs at each other and getting more
excited every minute at the thought of being able to sleep

together, and of all the fun we'd have before it was time for school in the morning.

We had got a fair way in front of Dickle's parents when Jacko and his best friend Billy caught us up.

'Why are you a-coming to ourn tonight, then?' Jacko asked as soon as they reached us. '*You* don't know, do you?'

I pretended not to notice, and went on running with Dickle, but Jacko persisted. 'Baby-cake Jed don't know, but I do! I do! I do! I know why! So there!'

Much as I disliked him, I felt that the circumstances were so very strange that perhaps there was something I didn't know and ought to find out. In spite of myself I stopped and listened.

'All right!' I said. 'Tell me why, if you're so clever.'

Dickle had come up and was standing beside me. Jacko looked up and down the road furtively and then came close enough to us to be able to whisper.

'Cos you Mam's going to 'ave a baby,' he said.

I was stunned. It was absolutely impossible – yet in some queer way I knew it was true.

Dickle recovered from the information before I could find my tongue.

'Jacko,' he said earnestly, 'where's the baby coming from? Where *do* babies come from?'

Their mother and some of her friends were getting dangerously near to us. Jacko returned to his old swaggering self.

'Where they all come from, silly-billy,' he said. 'From under old Mis' Harper's parsley bed, o' course' – and away he went, sniggering as usual, running at full speed to catch up Billy and a couple more big boys who were hanging over a gate looking at old Rouncer's pigs.

The Potts family lived in one of the tiny cottages, only one storey high, that were still scattered everywhere about the fens in my young days. It had had only two rooms, a house-place and a bedroom, at first, but a lean-to shed had been built on at the back. Half of this was now a back kitchen and the other half an extra bedroom where Jacko and Dickle slept. There was only just room in their bedroom for the double bed, and a door led from it into the back kitchen. Jacko was putting himself about and sulking so badly when we arrived that his father eventually boxed his ears and set him out to clean the mangolds for the cows before he could have his supper. Dickle's mother had understood how much Jacko's presence would spoil the treat of me and Dickle being together all night, so instead of putting us all three in the bed as we'd expected, she'd made a bed up on the floor of the house-place for Jacko.

Jacko was furious, but Dickle and I couldn't believe our good luck, and Jacko had no choice in the matter. He went to bed without speaking to either of us again, though he kicked Dickle's ankle enough to make him wince several times under the table while we were eating our bread and dripping supper. The whole family was in bed by ten o'clock, while it was still broad daylight, because Dickle's father had to be up at five o'clock to look after the animals on his own smallholding before going to work on another farm three miles away.

As soon as the door was shut between the main part of the cottage and our bedroom, Dickle and I went back to the subject that was uppermost in our minds – Jacko's news about my Mam.

'Do you really believe they come from under ol' Mis' Harper's parsley bed?' I asked.

Dickle considered the matter. 'Well,' he said, 'she's always there in a house where there is a baby, the next day. So I reckon she must *take* them, wherever they grow. Because one day I asked my Mam where they come from and she said God sent 'em. But she didn't say *how* he sent them. Perhaps he sends them to Mis' Harper, an' she keeps 'em under the parsley bed till they're ready to be took where they're ordered.'

That sounded sensible enough in one way, but it didn't explain a lot of things, like where the baby pigs came from, or

121

kittens, or calves, or puppies. Nobody had ever said *they* were found under the parsley as far as I had ever heard. But I did know very well that Mis' Harper, who could only walk with difficulty 'cos she had a bad leg and went dot-and-carry-one all the way, couldn't possibly have got round all the farms and smallholdings fast enough to take all them as well as babies. Besides, if it was so, why hadn't Dad answered Tod properly this morning? I said as much to Dickle.

'I wish we could find out for ourselves,' he said. 'If there's a lot of 'em under Mis' Harper's parsley it wouldn't take us long to dig one up, would it? Then we should *know*.' He started to get out of bed.

'What *now*?' I said, so startled at the very idea that I thought I must be dreaming.

'Why not?' said Dickle. 'We can get out o' the shed without 'em hearing us, an' there'll be a full moon. I heard Dad say so because he were on about all the people who'd be going home late after the Anni. Ol' Mis' Harper wont be there, 'cos she'll be gone up your house by now. Whether she takes 'em or not, she'll be there if your Mam is really having a baby, an' I reckon Jacko knows as she is.'

'I reckon she is an' all,' I said miserably, because I didn't want any change in our family at home. I wished we'd thought of digging the dratted baby out of the parsley bed before Mam had ordered it – though commonsense told me there'd be plenty more there. So it wouldn't have done any good.

Dickle had covered himself up again, and we lay there for a minute or two still talking, till Dickle's mother came and told us we had to go to sleep now, because our voices were keeping them awake. So we pretended to go to sleep, and watched the little square of window get darker and darker blue, until the moon rose and made the sky all silver again. Then Dickle said 'Come on, Jed' and got right out of bed. I'd never thought he really meant it till now, and I knew it was wrong. But I couldn't help being excited, all the same.

My heart beat so hard I thought Jacko must hear it in the next room and wake up, as we put our clothes on again – forgetting that they were the ones we'd had on for the Anni, and therefore our best. As we went through 'the shed' Dickle whispered 'We shall want some tools' and handed me his father's turf spade, which was bright as silver with wear, though it wasn't now used for turf digging. It still had an edge like a razor, but I was used to such implements and knew how to handle it. Dickle himself took a garden fork, and out we crept.

We went along the drove in the moonlight. There were a few cottages to pass between Dickle's home and the one a mile away where Mis' Harper lived. Dickle said we might be seen passing Mickey Bowd's house if anybody there was still up, so before we reached it we got into the dyke on the other side of the drove and went by the cottage in the shadow of the banks. It being mid-summer, the dyke was all but dry, though it was pretty muddy right down in the bottom.

It was getting on for midnight by the time we reached old Mis' Harper's, and we were quite a long time watching from the shelter of the dyke to make sure there were no lights in the cottage. We crept into the garden then, and up to the tiny house, and stood under the window we knew to be the old woman's bedroom. We listened and listened, hardly daring to draw breath, but there was no sound at all from inside.

'What did I tell you?' said Dickle. 'She's gone up your'n like I said.' So we went round the back, and found the parsley bed. It was only about a yard and a half square, full of lovely parsley. I said to Dickle, with some relief, that it didn't look as if it had been disturbed recently. But Dickle wasn't to be put off. (He was very much like Tod in a lot of ways. Perhaps that's why I got on so well with him.)

'You dig that side,' he said, 'and I'll dig this.' So we did. My digging was a very half-hearted affair, because my conscience was so guilty and I kept thinking what Dad would say when he found out. I had no doubt that he would find out. It seemed that both Mam and Dad always found out everything we ever did wrong. They always said that 'Miles's Boy' had told them. Once when Tod broke one of Mam's best cups, Dad took the pieces and threw them into the dyke down the fields so that Mam shouldn't know. But Miles's Boy told her, and Tod got the worst smacking she'd ever had. She said that night that if she ever got hold of that Miles's Boy she'd squash his thumbs and poke his eyes out, like the torture in the olden days, and then cut his tongue out so he could never tell anything about us ever again. The trouble was that we didn't know where to go to start looking for him.

I was thinking about him all the time we were digging. Every now and then my sharp spade would catch against something, and I'd hold my breath while I felt down with my fingers. But it always turned out to be a more-than-usually-tough parsley root. Dickle got his side properly dug over, but didn't find anything at all.

'Well, we've proved that to be a lie,' Dickle said, as we shouldered our tools and set off home again. 'Now we shall have to think out a way of finding the truth.'

We were cold and very tired, as well as a bit scared, by the time we'd cleaned the tools and put them back, and crept in to bed again. I wanted to wash, but Dickle said there was no water in the house and he wasn't going to the dipping hole at that time of night for anybody. So we snuggled down in a bed that smelt of parsley all over, it seemed to me, and were soon asleep.

We were so tired that Dickle's Mam had a real job to wake us in the morning, and we were in such a rush for school that there was no time even for Jacko to notice anything odd about us. We went from one drove across the planks over the dram to another drove and started up that one to the school, which was on the high road at the top of it. About half-way along the drove we met Tod and Dot coming across another lot of planks from Dot's house.

Tod was full of talk and chatter, ever so excited at having

had such a good time with Dot. She was still wearing her Anni clothes of course, but said that Dot's mother had told her to go home and change before school, because our teacher would understand if she was late. Tod said she wouldn't bother, because it would be lovely to be at school in her pretty new dress. But I warned her about Miles's Boy, and she said that perhaps she'd better do as she'd been told.

'What did you do last night, Jed?' she asked, and I felt as if I'd gone hot all over. It was just like a girl, especially Tod, to ask you the very question you didn't want to answer. I never did tell lies as a rule, especially to Tod. But I daren't tell her the truth this time, and I was wondering however I was going to get out of it when she went on, forgetting she'd ever asked me I think, in her eagerness to tell me what she and Dot had done.

'We played with Dot's dolls first,' Tod said, 'and Aunt Rose let me use the one she'd had when she was a little girl. Dot and me both said we wished we had a real baby at home to nurse, like Lucy Day and Maggie Leach always have. Aunt Rose said we should jolly soon wish we hadn't if we were always having the latest baby to cart round like they did. But she said we could wish for a baby without doing any harm, and told us how to do it. We had to go upstairs backwards with our eyes closed and sit on every step and wish for what we wanted most. When we got to the top we had to say 'Rabbits' and then not speak again at all until it was morning. Then as soon as ever we woke up in the morning we had to say 'Hares' before we said anything else, or our wish wouldn't come true. So we decided to do it.

'At the last minute, though, Dot said there were a lot of things she wanted more than a baby, and Aunt Rose said she was glad to know Dot was so sensible.' (Dot was listening to all this, but as usual when she was with Tod, she hardly said a word. She just kept nodding, to show that Tod was telling the truth. Dickle pretended not to be listening, but he liked Tod a lot, and I knew he was taking it all in as well.)

'Well,' Tod went on, 'we did exactly as Aunt Rose said, and said 'Rabbits' to each other at the top of the stairs. It was ever so hard not being able to speak to each other while we got undressed, and Dot pulled the button off her new shoes and said 'Drat the thing, where's it gone?' So I don't suppose she'll get her wish – but we sha'n't know till dinner time, 'cos she only wished she could get her sums right this morning. But I wished for a baby sister, and I never said a single word. And as soon as ever it was light and I opened my eyes, I remembered to say 'Hares' as loud as ever I could.'

Tod had hardly stopped talking for a second since we'd met her, and we were already near our own drove. It seemed there was plenty of time yet before school, so I decided I'd go on with Tod to our house, which was only about a quarter of a mile away. Dickle and Dot turned towards school, and Tod and I went on together. I was just wondering if I should tell her about what Jacko had said about Mam when we went by the last little house next but one to ours, where a nosey old woman named Mis' Margetts lived. She was at her gate as usual and as soon as ever we got near enough she called out 'Well, Tod, I suppose you're on your way home to see your new baby sister!'

I've never seen Tod look so flabbergasted and unbelieving before or since that moment. Her eyes opened till they looked like the dog's in the story of the Tinder Box, and though she kept on opening her mouth no words came out. Then she grabbed my hand and began to run, and we bolted down the last few yards to our gate as if we'd been shot out of a catapult.

When we burst through the door of the house-place, we stopped stunt, to take in the unaccustomed scene. Round the fire, drinking tea, was Grammam, looking very happy and satisfied, chatting to old Mis' Harper; and in Dad's chair on the other side of the fire was our beautiful Aunt Lizzie, holding a bundle in her arms wrapped in a long white shawl. I hung back and didn't know what to do or say. But Tod flew up to Aunt Lizzie and knelt down beside her and began pulling the shawl back to look at the baby. Aunt Lizzie let her, and nobody said anything.

Then Aunt Lizzie said; 'Come on, Jed. Come and look at her. She's your sister as well.' And I went. The baby was, as Grammam and Mis' Harper kept telling each other, 'as fat as butter' and 'like a child ten weeks old.' She had a fuzzy mop of jet black hair and round dark eyes so wide open that she looked like a baby owl. I knew straight away that however much I didn't want her I was going to love her. Tod took hold of her hand and she grabbed Tod's finger in her tiny fist and held on. But she seemed to be staring straight at me. I knew all the women were waiting for me to say something, but I was so shy I didn't know what to say.

Just then, the baby blinked, and looked more like a baby owl than ever, and I couldn't help laughing. But her pink plumpness made me think of the piglets Dad had taken up to show Tod only the morning before, and I said. 'She's just like a little tunky pig!' Then everybody laughed, and Aunt Lizzie said. 'That's just what she is' (because we always called a pig that was short from head to tail, and plump and well rounded, 'tunky'). But I didn't realise till a lot later on that I'd given my new little sister the nickname she would have to answer to all the days of her life, for 'Tunky' she still is. Aunt Lizzie told Dad what I'd said when he came in for his dockey, and he was so amused by it he started to call her Tunky from that very minute. And that was that.

And that should really be the end of the story, but it isn't. Mis' Harper went home later that day, and soon found what had happened to her parsley bed. People talked about it for days, and I didn't know where to put myself. Luckily for us, Mis' Harper's little house was quite near to the village pub, and everybody came to the conclusion that somebody had got drunk and dug the parsley bed up for a bet. Nobody could think of any other explanantion.

Then, later on that week, Dad drove over to a nearby village to see his old aunt, who lived with one of her daughters.

Next door to them lived another one of Dad's cousins, who had only got married last year. When he came back I heard him telling Mam that Cousin Sis's baby had come the night before and that he'd been able to bring Mis' Harper back with him in the trap to save her walking.

'Ah, it's a bad job,' he said, looking very sad and troubled. 'It's as beautiful a child as you ever see, apart from that. They do say as the doctors will be able to operate and make it so it don't show so much, but I'm sure I can hardly bear to think about it, especially when I look at our Tunky.' Then he said that old Aunt Betsy wanted very much too see Tunky and that he'd promised to take us all over to tea the next Sunday if Mam would like to go.

So we went, and before we'd been there long we had to go round and see Cousin Sis's new baby boy. She was holding him in a shawl, and as soon as ever she saw Mam holding Tunky she began to cry. Cousin John, her husband, tried to comfort her, and so did Mam, all saying that the clever doctors would put it right as soon as he was old enough, and so on. At last she opened the shawl and showed him to us. And there he was, as big and bouncy a baby as our own Tunky, but his top lip was cut into two parts, it seemed, and pulled and puckered up towards his nose. It made him terribly ugly, and horrible to look at.

I stared down at him with awful, *awful* fascination, for I knew now straight away what it was my sharp spade had touched when I'd been digging up Mis' Harper's parsley bed. I'd cut Cousin Sis's baby's lip, and all that sorrow and misery to them as well as to the poor baby, was all my fault. I'd known all the time I was doing wrong, too. That made it worse.

I don't know how I got through the rest of the day. I was so quiet, so near to tears, that they all teased me, even Dad, and said I was jealous because Tunky had put my nose out of joint. When I got to bed that night I prayed as I'd never prayed before, that God would make the doctors clever enough to be able to mend the baby's hare-lip, as they called it.

The next morning I was still so miserable that Mam thought I was sickening for something, and tried to give me some brimstone and treacle. But I fought her and ran off to school, crying. I couldn't bring myself to mention it to Dickle, so I stayed away from him, and he thought I didn't want to be friends with him any more, and went off with Sammy Iseley instead. Tod kept asking me what was the matter, and I told her to mind her own business; so, being Tod, she did. Then I really did feel like the leper in the Bible that everybody knew was 'unclean'. It went on for days, and I began to make myself really ill.

Then, the next Saturday night after I had gone to bed, Dad came upstairs. He came into my room and sat down on my bed, as he often did. Usually it made me feel wonderful, and grown-up, because we talked about all sorts of marvellous things before he went in to see Tod in her turn. But as soon as he sat down this Saturday night and spoke to me I started to cry. Then Dad picked me out of bed and wrapped the quilt round me, and cuddled me as if I had been Tunky.

'Now let's have it out what's it all about,' he said, and I told him. When I'd finished, he held me tight and kissed me and loved me as he would have done Tod, and I could feel him shaking as he held me close to his chest. I thought he was crying too, about what I'd done to that poor little baby, and I let out a long hopeless wail. Then I looked up, and Dad, who couldn't contain himself any longer, began to laugh, and laugh, and laugh till the tears did indeed run down his cheeks. When Tod put her head in to see what was the matter, he signalled to her to go away and stay away, and she had enough sense not to argue.

'Poor old Jed,' Dad said. 'It's all my fault you've been so worried. 'I ought to have told you long enough ago. To tell you the truth, I thought a boy like you, who've lived on a farm and played among other bigger boys all the time, couldn't help knowing all about it anyway. But your Mam, like all the rest of the silly women, is so dead set against children being told anything at all about such things, and I just went along with her to keep the peace. I ought to have had more sense! But when I think of you and Dickle digging up poor old Mis' Harper's parsley bed – ! I'm sorry you've been so worried, Jed, but it really does take the biscuit!' And off he went again, laughing till he had a job to get his breath.

Then when he'd had his laugh out he put me back into bed and told me about babies growing inside their mothers, till they were big enough and strong enough to come out, and that all babies, even our Tunky, had been born that way. Sometimes, he said, something went wrong and the poor baby was born with a hare-lip like Cousin Sis's baby. It was nobody's fault, and the doctors were getting cleverer at putting it right all the time.

He said he hadn't ever thought we'd believed the silly tales Mam and the other women told all children about babies being found under parsley beds or gooseberry bushes, or he would have told us the truth himself long ago.

Then he seemed to be making up his mind about something, and at last he said; 'Don't tell your Mam anything about it, Jed – not about the parsley bed, nor that you now know the truth. It would only upset her – and you may as well learn young that it's wiser not to ask for trouble where any woman's concerned. There's no need for Mam to know anything at all about it.'

'But Dad,' I said, 'if we don't tell her, Miles's Boy will! He always tells her everything!'

At this, Dad began laughing again, and I really thought he never would stop. Tod couldn't stay away any longer, and came creeping round the door to see what it was all about. I beckoned her to come into bed with me, and we joined Dad in his laughing, though Tod of course had no idea what it was all about. As soon as we stopped laughing to draw breath again, she asked to be let into the joke. Dad cocked his eyebrow up at me, asking me if he could tell Tod. I nodded, so he did.

When he'd gone through all the explanantion about babies again, I said, 'But what about Miles's Boy, Dad?'

He got up off the bed, and stood looking down at us. Then he went to the door, and stood holding it open. He seemed to be trying to find the right words, and we lay and waited, expectant of another startling revelation. But in the end, all he said was; 'I promise you that if *you* don't tell Mam somehow yourselves in the future, Miles's Boy will never be able to give you away to her again. Now work that out for yourselves.' Then he went away downstairs, still chuckling, to his Saturday night supper and his book.

And of course it didn't take Tod long to see what he meant. She always says that both of us really began to grow up from that minute onwards.

131

KILLING THE CAT

WE HAD TWO grandmothers, but only one grandad – Grandad Rattles. He and Grammam were Mam's and Aunt Lizzie's mother and father. Dad's mother we always called 'Grandmother', and it suited her, because she was strict and stern and very religious; so were her daughters, our other aunts, especially Aunt Harriet. They were all great chapel-goers, even Dad, and did everything by what it said in the bible. Well, at least, that's how it seemed to me and Tod.

Grandmother was a farmer. We had had a grandfather at the farm once, but I only just remembered him, and Tod couldn't, but we knew about him. Things had been very hard, and the farm hadn't been paying very well, Dad told us. Then one day poor old Grandad went out to do his yardwork, and found that all three of his horses had been in the barn, where the new wheat was. Of course, everybody knows that a pint of new wheat will kill a horse, especially if it's managed to get a drink afterwards. Grandad didn't know whether the horses had had much wheat, or whether they'd been at the horse-trough since. What he did know was that if he lost even one of them, he'd be ruined. As it happened, he'd caught them in time, and none of them died – but he did. The shock was so great it brought on a heart attack, and he died next day. Then grandmother went on farming, with Dad's help. He was her horsekeeper, and she paid him just his week's wages and not another penny, although, of course, he did everything, and took all the responsibility, though none of the profit. His mother kept the reins in her hands, and at the time I'm telling you about, she was coming up to eighty.

Now we knew all about this, because Mam had a lot to say

in front of us, on the subject of Dad's family. They didn't get on any too well together a lot of the time, though there were other times when it was all honey instead of all the other thing; but Dad's family were looked up to because they were such honest, God-fearing and chapel-going folk, and they were very set against Dad marrying Mam in the first place.

The trouble was that Mam came from a very different sort of family. Grandad Rattles was Irish to the bone, though he'd been born in the fen. Mam's family were as poor as church mice, because Grandad was the black sheep of the whole neighbourhood. He never worked if he could help it, or if he could get money any other way, and some folks said he didn't care how. He was for ever in some trouble or other with the police or his neighbours, for poaching or doing them down somehow, besides having a terrible temper that got him into all sorts of other difficulties. He liked his beer, and spent a tidy lot of his time at *The Ram*, or *The True Briton*, or *The Golden Drop*, where the gift he had of spinning long yarns without a word of truth in them didn't do much to help his character in the eyes of such people as Dad's mother and sisters. The result was that if he did happen to hit on the truth by mistake, that was enough to make everybody else who knew him swear the opposite. All the same, he was a tall, strong, handsome man with charm enough to fool anybody who didn't know him, as a lot of folks found out to their cost. But I loved him, and he loved me, though he never did like Tod.

Of course, the one who suffered most from all his goings on was Grammam. (We both loved her a hundred times more than we did Grandmother.) She had to earn what living they had, by going out washing or potato-setting and so on. She had to get him out of all his scrapes, and put up with all his rampages, and there's no doubt she had a terrible life with him. But she was such a sweet, gentle, good-natured, merry sort of woman that if there was a chance to be happy for five minutes she'd take it; and when Mam went on about Grandad, and what a disgrace he was to us all, she'd stick up for him, and scold Mam for it.

'Now then!' she'd say. 'Remember who you're talking about, my gal. Whatever he is, he's your father, and you know what the commandmant says: Honour thy father an' thy mother'. Then Mam would sulk, and say she wasn't going to honour that old humbug, whatever the bible said; and she just didn't know how Grammam could put up with him, and why she didn't leave him for good and come and live with us.

'I'm got more sense than that, my gal' Grammam would say. 'Visitors and fish stink after three days' keepin! Besides, them as 'as mad bulls to deal with know best how to deal with 'em. I made my bed, and now I's'll have to lay on it. He's my 'usband, after all.'

So Dad's mother and sisters never lost a chance of reminding Mam that they were a cut above her and her family, especially her 'old jail-bird' of a father. (This was coming it a bit too strong, I thought, because the only time he'd actually been in jail was for stealing a cat from a pub. He'd took a fancy to it, and made off with it – but the landlady was as much of a cat lover as he was, and he had a month in jail over it.)

There's no doubt Mam was ashamed of him; but the funny thing was that apart from that, she thought herself a notch or two above our other aunts who'd never been out of the fen. Mam and Aunt Lizzie, both of them so pretty and well-behaved (so Dad said) that everybody who saw them fell in love with them, went off to service as parlourmaids in a rich Quaker-man's house in Nottingham, but they weren't there long enough to learn their job. Mam got whisked off as a companion to a queer, rich old woman (she was my god-mother, but it didn't do me much good), and Aunt Lizzie became housekeeper to a bachelor doctor and his aristocratic old mother. The doctor fell in love with her, and wanted to marry her, but his mother wouldn't let him. So he never got married, and took to drink. Aunt Lizzie married somebody else of her own station, and then they both went and lived with the doctor, and looked after him till his mother died and he drank himself to death.

So they'd been used to folks doing things proper – like speaking proper and having good table manners. They both had different ideas about dressing themselves, and us, and were very set on me and Tod knowing how to behave ourselves. The other women said they 'di'n't know which way their behinds hung', and called them 'dink-me-dolls'. But what aggravated Grandmother and our aunts most was that Mam had made it quite clear in the first place that she wouldn't go out to work in the fields, except perhaps making bands at harvest time, or live like the other women expected to. 'I married your son to keep me' she'd say to Grandmother, when she got on to her high horse, 'and I'll see to it that he does'. There's no doubt Grandmother aggravated Mam to be a lot more extravagant than she might have been. She was always telling Mam off for buying this or getting the other, and spending 'Bill's money'. Then Mam would flush up, and show she was Rattles's daughter. Her beautiful black eyes would flash, and she'd say 'As long as God gives him strength to earn it, I hope he'll give me strength to spend it!'

Then there'd be a real row, and we hated that, because it made Dad so miserable; but it would soon blow over, and they'd get on like a house afire again. Not Grandad Rattles, of course. He wasn't welcome at the farm – not that he wanted to go. He always called Grandmother 'the bloody old Wisewoman', though Dad couldn't do wrong for him, and Dad actually liked the old rapscallion, even if he didn't like the things he got up to.

But there was no doubt about it – Dad did work too hard, what with his job at the farm, and his own small-holding, and the job at the mill. In spite of that, he always seemed to have time for us, and we saw a lot more of him than most of our school mates ever saw of their fathers. All the men in the fen had to work like distraction, as Dad always said, to keep their families fed; but most of them found enough money to spend their evenings in the pubs, and they expected the children to be in bed before they got home. Then they were up and away again by five o'clock in the morning, before the kids were up. Their wives got up to get their breakfasts, looked after pigs and poultry, dug the gardens, went out to work in the fields, and got home again in time to have the pudden' cooked by half-past three in the afternoon when the horses were un-yoked. Then when the father had finished work, all the family worked on their own patch of land till the man went to the pub and the children to bed (though there was usually a bit of playtime for them after the pigs had been fed and the mangolds cleaned for next day, and so on).

By the time Tunky was born though, Dad had worked himself into something called 'a nervous breakdown'. It had the sort of sound about it that Tod loved, but we didn't like anything else about it, I can tell you. For one thing, it had upset his heart. It had begun to act queer, – jumping about, he said, and missing beats, and running down like a chain slipping cog. It would start doing it without any reason or warning, and of course we all thought he was going to die every minute. But sometimes it would do it for hours (even days) on end, and we didn't need telling when it was bad. You see, as I've said before, he always sat cross-legged, with the leg that had been broke on the top. Then his dangling foot, turned slightly at the wrong angle, picked up his pulse, and jerked with it. When his 'old heart was bad', as he used to say, we used to watch that foot like birds watching a snake, 'One-two-three-------FOUR!   One-two-three-four------FIVE! One-two---------THREE! We could actually see the beats, see the long pauses, see the thump. We watched for him to die in front of our eyes. No wonder, come to think of it, that we didn't take in anything else that was happening, that summer. (I think I ought to explain that our doctor had told Dad there was nothing he could do to cure the heart complaint; but he had neglected to explain that it wasn't a particularly dangerous condition – only a very uncomfortable one. Dad lived to be eighty – and all three of us inherited his extra-systole, Tod worse than me or Tunky. If we'd known then what we know now, we shouldn't have spent so many hours of anguished apprehension.) But I must get back to my tale.

As soon as Dad began to go back to work again, the pattern of our lives changed. Grandmother had at last decided to give up the farm. She was looking for somewhere else to live 'come Michaelmas', and Dad and Mam spent a lot of time talking about something called a 'capital redemption policy'. This didn't worry us much because Tod said if anything was 'capital' that meant it was alright. Uncle Jim always said 'Tha's capital!' when he was pleased with anything. We took in enough to understand that we were going to move house in the autumn, and live in Grandmother's 'on the high road', close to the school; but nobody ever explained to us that Mam had got her way at last, and that Dad was going to buy the farm from Grandmother. We simply thought Dad was going to work for the new farmer, whoever it was.

In the meantime, to save Dad a lot of extra work and journeys, because he still wasn't at all well, we spent all our days up at the farm, and only slept down the drove.

It was a queer, in-between sort of time, and lasted all one summer. It seems funny to me, now, looking back on it, that we – Tod and me – didn't take in what was happening, but we just didn't. We had been used to going up there for long days all during the harvest time, since we could walk. It was – or seemed to us – only a sort of extra long harvest. Mam put Tunky, and all our food for the day, in the pram, and we went off early enough for us to get to school.

In the afternoon, we went back to Grandmother's house, and stopped there till Dad had finished work before going back home down the drove. We didn't see much of Grandmother. She kept to 'the front room' a lot of the day, and we kept to the back kitchen and 'the house-place'.

Of course, Tod and me didn't care. We had always loved being round the yard with Dad, when he was baiting his horses, and doing the yardwork; and he never seemed to think we were in his way, or hindering him. We would trail round at his heels peeling pig potatoes while they were still hot, dipping them in pollard and eating them. We loved to turn the handle of the mangold-pulper, and watch the long, thin, orange and yellow strips come tumbling out of it. When we'd finished the potatoes, we chose the cleanest, longest strip of mangold, and ate that, as a second course, before finishing our treat with a lump of crunchy linseed cattle-cake. We climbed into the chaff-house and buried each other in chaff, pulling it all over us till Tod's hair was full of it and I had to take my shoes and stockings off to get rid of it. The barn smelled like paradise ought to, I thought, with a mixture of wheat and sacks and tar-cord and cattle-cake and a dozen more things all mixed up together; and best of all was the straw-stack, a huge stack of last year's straw with one straight side from which a load was cut every day to straw the bullock yard. By summer, the straw stack would have got low enough for us to be allowed to play on providing we kept away from the place where the huge-bladed cutting knife was left sticking in the straight, cut side. We would bounce about on top as much as we liked, slide down on a chute made of the slippery stuff to a huge bed of loose straw at the bottom, crawl under the heavy stack-cloth that kept the stack dry, or burrow tunnels into the bottom of it. Apart from the danger of the knife, which we perfectly well understood, no restrictions were put on our use of the straw-stack as a playground, not even by Grandmother herself.

Then there were the animals – the three horses that we knew by name and character, as if they were people, and Grandmother's slow old pony, Bess. (There was tale that one day in winter our Grammam was walking to Ramsey, round by the road because the fields were too wet. Grandmother with Bess in the buggy came along behind her, and stopped to speak to her about something. When the business was done, Grandmother said 'Will you ride, Mis' Papworth?' and without thinking, Grammam replied 'No, thank you all the same Mis' Edwards. I'm in a hurry'.)

There were pigs with piglets of different sizes, hens with fluffy chickens, ducks with ducklings, and geese with goslings; when there was a new born calf to be seen, it was almost too much to bear, for the sight and feel of the curly, liver and chocolate coat, and the bright blue eyes and the pert little ears were so beautiful that it hurt you, down somewhere inside where you couldn't get at it to rub the place better. Then Dad would bring the bucket of warm milk, and we knew just how to cup our hands enough to make a hollow, and offer the calf our fingers to suck so that it got the milk. Tod used to cry, sometimes, to hear the cow calling for it, and while I took my turn feeding it she'd stroke it and kiss its wet little muzzle, and press the waves in its coat into lines with her fingers.

And of course, every now and then, we'd hear a strange sort of throaty mew coming from a manger or an old wheelbarrow full of sacks, and find a cat had had a litter of kittens. That was the very peak of all, because all of us were dotty about cats.

We had a strain of white cats with black patches on them – smooth-haired and sleek, with greeny-yellow eyes. They were wonderful hunters, and lovely as pets. A year or so before, the one we had down the drove had produced three kittens. Dad had taken one up to Grandmother when it was old enough, and we had kept two – but we still regarded the one up at the farm as ours, and grudged him having to leave us. The two left, Dad named Kitchener and Jellicoe, after the famous general and admiral of the time. Jellicoe came to a sad end, because one morning when Dad was putting his boots on in the shed, he stood his lighted candle on the floor, and Jellicoe came up and took a sniff at the flame. He died in a minute – but Dad didn't get over it for years. He was really soft about animals, in spite of being a farmer. If a mouse squeaked and looked at him when it was rushing away in fright, he couldn't kill it; he had to let it go. The terror in its eyes would haunt him, he said. (The funny thing to me now is that none of his fellow farmers and neighbours ever regarded him as 'soft' or 'daft'. On the contrary, they all looked up to him, went to him for help, and told each other the funny things he'd said, and what 'a cure' he was.)

So we were left with 'Kitch', who turned out to be a lady; but her brother up at the farm was also called 'Kitch', like every other one of the same colouring for donkey's years afterwards. We adored 'farm Kitch' as much as our own, 'home Kitch'.

There had been one change that had started in the spring, when Dad was too bad to work at all. A man called Ben Munsey, who had been a labourer on the farm for years, had had to take over the horses and the yardwork, or most of it and even when Dad went back to work, this change went on. Ben Munsey (Mr. Munsey to us, of course) lived in a tiny house the other side of the farmyard, across the pond, with his wife and no end of children. I forget how many there'd be at the time I'm writing about, but I guess six or seven. The oldest was a girl called Edie, who was just about Tod's age. Tod missed Dot a lot, that summer we spent up at the farm before we actually went to live there, and she tried to make friends with Edie. But Edie could never come to play without having three or four younger ones with her, and the baby on her arm. Then they'd all stand there in a row, just looking, as if they didn't know how to play. We soon found out why.

Tod and me were playing on the straw stack one day after school. I had just given Tod a shove off to send her sliding down to the heap of straw at the bottom of the stack, and was waiting for my own turn, when a bellow from the cut side stopped me in my tracks. I can still remember looking down at Tod as she sprawled in the straw, staring up at Ben Munsey. Her eyes were nearly sticking out like chapel hat-pegs with surprise and fright, and she sort of froze with her legs up in the air and her knickers showing. Grandmother would have been scandalised.

'What d'yer reckon you're up to, you young 'umbug?' he bawled. 'Clear off back to the 'ouse, an' don't you let me catch you round my stacks no more! D'yer 'ear me? Clear orf!'

We did, very puzzled; but from that time on, we found a lot more of our old pleasures barred to us. In fact, we were not welcome in the yard any longer. Harvest and the holidays had come, and for the first time Dad let me lead the empty carts up to the stackyard and back to the field. I felt I was a man, helping with the work at last. There was no time for me to play – at least, not much. So Tod was left by herself a good deal, and she did her best to get Edie to play with her.

Ben Munsey was always tearing about as if his very life depended on getting the next load of sheaves stacked. He was a tall, thin, wiry man, with a hawk-face dried to a reddish-brown with the sun and the wind. He drove everybody to work as hard and as fast as he did himself, so that even Dad himself grumbled occasionally. The weather was very hot – real harvest weather – but it had turned thundery all of a sudden and the men had begun to worry that there might be a storm. Mr. Munsey had kept us all at it with only a few minutes' break for dockey, and at tea-time we had had to knock off for the yardwork to be done and the helpers to have a meal, though we should start again and keep at work till it was too damp to bring in any more corn. I was tired, but when I'd had my tea I wandered off to find Tod. She was in the empty cart-hovel, playing 'houses' with Edie and the rest of the Munsey tribe.

Tod had set out her treasures – old bits of crockery she pretended were cups and saucers – and they were about to take a 'pretend' tea. As soon as I came in sight, Tod told me I could be the chapel minister visiting on a Sunday, and say grace for us all. I was just trying to remember the grace the preacher always said, when Mr. Munsey came down on us 'like Moses down the mountain' Tod said afterwards.

He kicked the bits of crockery flying, and took Edie by her hair and dragged her to her feet. All the others scrambled up looking so 'frit' that they never uttered a sound. Tod got up as well, and came close to me for protection, though I didn't feel very brave. Ben looked down at the row of his own children, and clouted every one in turn except the baby, who cried anyway as soon as all the others started. Tod and I stood waiting our turn – Tod nearly crying already, what with fright and apprehension and disappointment (Mam slapped us now and then, but we weren't used to anybody really hitting us). We never took our eyes off Mr. Munsey, but instead of boxing our ears, he turned his attention back to his own brood, and I was afraid he was going to give them all a second go round. He raised his hand, and said 'Now then! DRY UP!' They had all been blaring and bleating fit to deafen you, but the moment he spoke, every one of them gulped, snuffled, swallowed, and stopped in mid-grizzle, just like that. Not another sound came from the whole row.

It was so funny that I was afraid I was going to laugh and more afraid that Tod would, because she'd caught hold of my arm and I could feel her trying not to giggle, though she was really still shaking with fright and temper. Then Mr. Munsey simply jerked his head sideways towards the big farm gate, and away all his brood went, trailing after Edie like ducklings down to the water. When he jerked his head in the opposite direction, towards the house, we were glad enough to get away.

As soon as we were out of earshot, Tod turned to look back. Munsey was harnessing a horse to a cart, with his back to us. Tod put her tongue out as far as she could, and said 'I *hate* him! And I shall tell Dad!'

'It won't do any good!' I said. 'You know Dad never goes against anything he says or does. I did tell him one day last week when Mr. Munsey had turned us out o' the barn, and all he said to me was to keep out of his way, 'cos 'e didn't like children. Couldn't abide 'em, Dad said. And now 'e was the horsekeeper, it'd perhaps be better not to be round the yard when he was doing the work.'

'Is he the horsekeeper – really?' asked Tod.

'Tha's what Dad said. An' I 'eard 'im telling Mam that 'e reckoned Ben's wife 'ould be glad o' the extra money, with all that tribe o' kids. He told Mam there was going to be another soon – another baby, he meant. And Dad laughed, and said "Abou Ben Munsey, may his tribe increase" – like that bit of poetry we had to learn at school, and you'd been reciting to Dad. But Mam said it was a disgrace, 'cos Nellie Munsey had been such a fine girl before she'd married him. I reckon they'd forgot I was there.'

Tod looked very puzzled and worried. 'Jed' she said. 'If Mr. Munsey is the horsekeeper now, what's Dad?'

We looked at each other. There was only one explanation. Dad had been the boss's son until now, but he'd been ill and couldn't work so hard. He'd had to change places with Ben Munsey.

I was quite old enough to realise that there must be a flaw in this argument somewhere; but the more I thought about it, the more it was clear to me that Dad *never* did do anything to contradict or disagree with Ben Munsey. Ben would be issuing orders in the morning now like a serjeant-major, and Dad would just be there, getting on with his work, whistling or saying nothing. As we went towards the house, though, I made up my mind that if Tod didn't ask him, I would, soon as I could. Tod had got her chin stuck out, now, though, and I knew her too well to doubt that she'd march straight in and pour out the tale of her wrecked tea-party. So perhaps we should soon know the truth, however bad it was.

As it happened, there was such a commotion going on in the house-place when we got there, that it drove everything else straight out of our heads. Dad had been taking a cat-nap on the hearthrug, when his heart had suddenly 'started its ticks', and just would not get right again. It had woke him up, and what with the heat and the hard work he'd been doing all day when he'd tried to sit up, he'd turned dizzy. He'd fallen back again on the rug, and started to hit his chest with his fist, over where his heart was.

When we went in, Mam was on her knees beside him, shouting at him as if he was deaf, and saying 'Bill! Bill! Are you alright? O dear, what shall I do? Harriet, Harriet! What shall we do?' (Our Mam never was much good in an emergency.)

Tunky was in her high chair, squealing like a pig having its throat cut, and Aunt Harriet who'd come by chance to see Grandmother, was standing beside Tunky saying 'Shush! There, now, that'll do. 'Old yer row. Shush, there's a good child!' She got hold of Tunky to lift her out of her chair, but Tunky let out such a squeal that Aunt Harriet dropped her again, and left her to yell, while she went and stood over Dad, as well.

Grandmother was lifting up her apron, and her skirt, to fumble in the pocket she always wore on a tape round her waist, between her top petticoat and her skirt. After what seemed a hundred years to us, she produced a key, went to the mahogany chiffonier at the side of the room, and unlocked one of the doors. From it she took a bottle of brandy and an egg-cup. She filled the egg cup as if she were giving out the communion wine at chapel, and handed it to Aunt Harriet, just like the minister handing down one of the little glasses the grown ups 'took the sacrament' in. Aunt Harriet handed it down to Mam, and Mam, still trembling and crying, sloshed it up against Dad's lips. He grabbed it from her, tipped his head back and swallowed the brandy – there wasn't much more than a thimbleful. Then he said 'Can't any of you numbskulls see that that poor child's got her foot wedged in her chair?' And he sprang to his feet and took two strides to where Tunky was, to ease her fat little ankle from where she'd got it stuck between the footboard and the leg.

147

Then all the women started talking at once, telling everybody else what had happened (as if they didn't know already), while Dad comforted Tunky, and Tod and me stood like mice, nearly unable to believe he was still alive and apparently well. The women all said he mustn't think of going back to work again that night; and he agreed that there was going to be a storm anyway, and we had better get off home down the drove before it started. Aunt Harriet went with us, because our house was on her way, and Dad carried Tunky on his shoulders while I wheeled his bike. He seemed his usual self, but the rest of us couldn't get over the fright half so well.

The storm came, and for the next day or two Mam and us children didn't go up to the farm. When we did go again, the next Monday, the holidays were over, and we had to go back to school again.

Of course, at school I didn't see much of Tod. The girls sat on one side of the big room, and the boys the other, and at playtime we each had our own yards. We weren't allowed to speak to each other through the railings, on pain of being caned. Tod was always good at her lessons, and I wasn't too bad myself, so I never had to watch her being caned, or she me, for not doing her work properly, like some brothers and sisters had to. Our teacher, Miss Cornell, was very strict, but she didn't often cane girls – only when they were rude to her. But the boys had to hold out their hands for every word spoke in school, or every blot, or every page of sums they got wrong. Miss Cornell was a good teacher in her way, though, and Tod loved her. I didn't. I was frightened at her, and of her swishing cane. I'd seen what it could do to your fingers, and heard boys my own size cry all the way home after a stroke on each hand. I think I hated Miss Cornell; but I'd got Grandad Rattles's secret promise that if ever she caned me he'd go up and thrash her with her own cane till she'd never sit down comfortable, or play the 'pianny' again. I knew he'd never do it, but it comforted me, all the same. And in this, for once, Dad was on my side rather than Tod's. He didn't quarrel with

148

her way of keeping discipline, though I really don't know what he'd have done if she had ever caned any of us, and he backed her up in what she tried to do for our education. But all the same, he had two things against her. One was that when a farm labourer – say a horsekeeper – worked seven days a week for eighteen shillings (or at the most £1) rumour had it that she got £5 for five days, and all holiday times when she wasn't at work, as well. He could not see reason or justice in that; and the other was, that she was neither a Conservative or a Liberal, but called herself a Socialist, and let it be known that she believed in a man called Ramsey something or other. Naturally, we thought whoever he was must come from our Ramsey, with a name like that, and couldn't see why Dad should be so set against him! But when we asked him what he meant, all he'd say was that if Miss Cornell was a Socialist, she should practice what she preached. Five pounds a week for five days from nine till half-past-three, and only two out of every three weeks in the year at that! It was, he said, easy enough to have big ideas about all folks being equal, when you'd got a job like she had.

It was all beyond me, anyway. All I wanted was to be old enough to leave school and forget it, but Mam was always going on at me about going to some other school at Ramsey, called the Grammar School. Not if I could help it; but I didn't worry much because only the very clever children went there, and them whose folks could afford to pay for them. Farm labourers' children were usually safe enough from it. And anyway, Grandad Rattles had said he'd see to it that I didn't have to go to such foolery as learning grammar and that.

When we went back to school after the summer holidays I'm telling you about, poor Tod was in for a shock. Ever since she'd been at school, she'd sat next to Dot; but Dot was away with scarlet-fever, and wouldn't be back for six weeks or more. Miss Cornell shuffled the new class round, and Dot's place by Tod's side was soon occupied by Edie Munsey. Well, as Tod said, Edie wasn't Dot, but she was her new friend, and our new boss's daughter. It might have been worse. All the same, Tod grieved for Dot, and was exasperated by Edie, who was such a slow-coach at her lessons that even Tod lost patience, trying to help her. In the end she gave up, so usually Edie sat and cried, sniffling quietly, because she couldn't do her sums, while Tod romped through hers like a hot knife through butter.

So I come at last to the point of this long talk. I've been going round by Bill's mother's to get there, I know. We'd got to the end of September, and the threshing tackle had been booked to come, so that threshing could start on Monday morning. We were always so excited we didn't know what to do, when the great steam engine, pulling the drum and the jack-straw behind it, pulled into the yard and sidled up to the cornstacks. They usually came in the evening, when the men's faces would all be coal black after a day's work; then they positioned everything ready for the next day. We watched from far off, because we were warned of the danger – but Mam would come sometimes, and stop with us. When the whole threshing tackle was actually at work, we used to stand and chant:-

'Digger Dugger, Soap and Sugar, Digger Dugger Soap and Sugar'. That's what mothers always told their babies the engine said.

On this occasion, the tackle had arrived on Saturday. On Monday morning we set off very early, so as to have plenty of time to see the engine before we went to school. Dad had been gone hours, because it took a long time to get steam up after a weekend and the farm men always had to do that before the engine driver and his team arrived. Mam had said we'd be up there early enough to have our breakfasts with Dad for once, just before the threshing-tackle team arrived for them to start work.

Mam set the breakfast, and Dad came in and sat down. Tod was sitting by him, as she always did, but I wanted to look at that engine. I just couldn't eat till I had done, and when Mam wasn't looking, I slipped out. I don't know if Dad saw me go, but if he did, he didn't let on. I went straight round to the stacks, with one wary eye open for Ben Munsey, but I couldn't see a soul anywhere, so I stood and gazed my fill, walking round and round the engine and thinking how much I'd love to drive it, like old Jimmy Roberts, who'd soon be here now to start it working. I thought I'd just take a look round the drum and jackstraw, when from out between them came Ben Munsey, and my stomach sort of dropped out of place, partly because I was frightened, but also because he was carrying something white in his hands. My heart nearly stopped beating and I could see straight away that it was 'Farm Kitch'. I could tell at a glance that Kitch was very dead. Munsey slung him down by the cornstack.

'Bloody ol' cat' he said. 'Must a' went into the drum arter a mouse, I reckon. I were just turning the beaters b' 'and, to see if they were free, an' felt a thump. It 'ad 'ad 'im, broke 'is neck, most like.'

I grabbed poor old Kitch up in my arms, still warm and limp, and ran towards the house. I knew he was dead, but all the same I had to get him to Dad as quick as I could, just in case there was anything he could do. I broke into the house-place blubbering, and holding Kitch up to my face as if I could love him back to life. Dad jumped up, and took him from me, but laid him down again straight away and came to comfort me. I hid my face in his shirt, and cried and cried. Tod was sobbing as if her heart would break, and Mam was trying to comfort her, though we were both beyond all comfort. Mam was wiping her own tears away as well as Tod's, and when I finally lifted my face up to look at Dad, I could see he was having a job with his own face.

'How did it happen?' he said, as soon as I could speak. I told him what Mr. Munsey had said. He sat down again at the table without another word and began again on his breakfast. Mam tried to get me to eat, but every time I put something in my mouth, I'd take a look at Kitch's limp body and choke before I could swallow. Dad was just about to get up and go out to start work, when a tap came at the door, and there stood our old neighbour from the farm across the road. He came in, and was told why all of us were so miserable.

Mr. Harlock took off his cap, gazing at poor old Kitch all the time, and scratching his head.

'D'yer say Ben were turning the beaters *by 'and*?' he said unbelievingly, to Dad. Why man – as soon as that ol' cat 'ad felt 'em move, it 'ould a-bin out o' that drum like greased lightnin! Besides, as soon as they started to pinch, it 'ould a-squalled murder loud enough for folks to 'ear it at Ramsey!'

The two men looked at each other, eye to eye, over the white body of our departed pet. Tod and I had both stopped crying, and were looking at them as if we knew that something specially important was about to happen. I can still feel that sort of awed, fascinated feeling in the pit of my stomach now, after all these years, when I think about it. Then Dad spoke, slow, and stern and angry, in a voice so cold I hardly recognised it.

'Alty' he said 'if I thought Ben Munsey killed our ol' cat a-purpose, I'd go straight out into the yard this minute, and sack him on the spot, threshing or no threshing!'

'You'll never prove it', Alty was answering – but Tod and I didn't wait for any more. We just made for the door, and went out down the garden, wondering. We didn't speak. What with Kitch dead and the revelation we'd just heard, we couldn't find words. Ben Munsey had killed Kitch just on purpose – just because he felt like it, just because he didn't like cats perhaps, any more than he liked children; that was stupefying enough in its own right. But then Dad had said *he would go straight out and sack Ben*. That could only mean one thing. Dad was now the farmer – that's why Ben Munsey was the horsekeeper. The bits all fell into place like a bit of string comes out of a knot as soon as you pull the right end. I was relieved that I quite forgot poor Kitch's limp little body in my arms, though Tod kept sobbing on and off. She was still crying when we got to school, and Edie was waiting for her.

Now I shall have to go back back a bit to say that our Aunt Lizzie, who had no children of her own, was very clever with her needle, and her sewing machine. She lived in a town that had a weekly market, and when she could, she bought pretty bits of material and made them into frocks for Tod. In the spring of that year, she had come one day, and brought about four cotton frocks with her, which Tod had been wearing all the summer. One of them was a white one, with little black golliwogs all over it, and this was Tod's favourite of all her frocks. When we'd started back to school after the holidays, we had both had new school clothes, ready for the autumn. But now the weather had turned hot again, and the night before the tragedy, Tod had asked Mam if she could wear her golliwog frock next day. Mam had said no, and Tod had made a fuss, and they'd had a real battle of wills and words, during which I'd heard Mam say in exasperation that she didn't know now where it was, and anyway Tod had grown so much it wasn't big enough for her. So Tod had had to give in. Now, as we neared school, with Tod still sobbing from the tragedy behind us, and me in a sort of dazed state from the sudden revelation of the reality of things, good as well as bad, Edie Munsey came running towards us, *wearing Tod's golliwog dress.*

Tod let out a wail and a sob, and dashed into the playground, pushing Edie out of the way, and mouthing 'Go away! *I hate you!*' as she passed. Unfortunately for her, Miss Cornell had just come out to ring the bell, and saw it all happen. She pursed her lips and scowled after Tod, while I stood there wishing I dare go into the girls' playground to comfort Tod. I took my cap off, and went to the gate, very scared, but full of a new confidence born of the knowledge that I was now (or very nearly) the son of a farmer.

'Please Miss' I said. 'Our cat's been squashed in the threshing tackle. That's why Tod's crying.'

'Thrashing, not threshing' she corrected me (quite

wrongly, of course. It muddled me for years). 'That is sad, but I don't suppose it was Edie's fault. Get into your own proper playground.'

I did. Tod and Edie had to sit side by side in school but Tod turned away from her as much as she could, still sobbing every time she looked at the golliwog dress. She said afterwards it wasn't because she cared so much about Edie having the dress, as the fact that the black and white reminded her of Kitch. I could see what she meant.

When we went home to dinner, Kitch had been buried, and Dad promised us that after we'd moved, or perhaps even before, 'Home Kitch' would have some kittens, and we could keep one each of them. Tod wiped her eyes and washed her face, and Mam explained that the Munseys were very poor, because of there being so many of them; so when she had been clearing things out, ready to move house on October 11th, she had sorted out all the clothes we'd grown out of to give to Mrs. Munsey. She hadn't expected Edie to wear them till next summer, when Tod couldn't possibly have got into them anyway. And Dad explained that Ben Munsey was a very queer man in many ways, but he was the best worker in the fen, and we were lucky to have him, really; but when the threshing was over, he'd have a word with him about Kitch, and all our other cats, so that nothing like this ever happened again.

So off we went back to school in the afternoon, reconciled to the world. Tod and Edie were soon playing hopscotch together, and I saw that all was well. I forgot them, till the bell rang and we yelled 'All in! All in! All in!' as we began to line up at the door.

The first lesson of the afternoon was history, and then we came to *English*. Miss Cornell took a lot of the words that had been in the lesson in our history book, and wrote them up on the blackboard. Then she told us to write sentences, and each sentence was to have in it one word from the board, to show we understood what the word meant. Tod seized her pen and began to write. She loved words, and would have ten sentences done while the rest of us were struggling with one. Which word should I choose? Realm? Nephew? Royal? Servant? Impostor? Scullion? Foreign? None of them seemed to have much to do with me. I'd decided on 'scullion', because it seemed the easiest, and wrote 'When old onions grow shoots they are called scullions and we eat them.' I was struggling with 'Nephew' when Miss Cornell said 'Pens down. Arms folded. Who has done all ten?'

Up shot Tod's hand – the only one.

'Good girl, Tod' said Miss Cornell. 'Come out to the front, and read your sentences to the class.'

Out went Tod with her book, and began to read, while Miss stood there with a pleased expression on her face, as if whatever Tod read out, all the praise was due to her, and not to Tod at all. I glared at her, thinking how much I hated her. Tod began.

'King George is the king of this realm.'

'Good girl!' nodded Miss.

'My brother Jed is my Aunt Lizzie's nephew.'

'*Very* good,' said Miss, while I blushed and squirmed because everybody turned round and looked at me.

'The king's family are called the royal family.'

'Is, not are' said Miss. Nobody understood that but Tod coloured all the same, because she gathered she had somehow made a mistake.

'Go on' said Miss.

'Mr. Munsey is my father's servant.'

Miss turned red, and then white. '*What?*' she said. 'Read that again! What have you written?'

'Mr. Munsey is my father's servant.'

'How *dare* you write such a wicked thing!' said Miss, boxing Tod's ear hard. 'You nasty, spiteful, horrid girl! Give me your book!' Tod, too surprised and bewildered to cry, handed her the book. Miss took it, and tore out the offending page.

155

'See' she said. 'This is what happens to work that cannot be left for the inspectors to see! I shall tell them when they come why a page has been torn out from your book.'

She tore the page into a dozen fragments, and dropped them into the coal bucket as if they had something nasty on them. Then she turned back to Tod, who by this time had begun to sob again.

'Never let me hear you call anyone your servant again' she said 'you nasty, spoiled, pampered child! It is not Edie's father's fault that he has to work hard to keep your father rich enough to buy a farm! You are all equal in God's sight, every one of you. I will not allow those who come from farms to look down on those who come from cottages! Those who work together on farm-land should all have the same rewards. None should be better off than any other. The time will come when nobody will own land, and every one will have to be satisfied with a labourer's wage. That will cure nasty little snobs calling good men her *servants*.' This, and much, much more that I can't remember now. Tod was now crying so terribly that I was whimpering myself. We'd never seen Miss like this before, with anyone, let alone Tod.

Miss suddenly shook Tod, and then said. 'Edie, come out here.' Edie trembled, but went.

'Tod' said Miss 'I thought Edie was your friend; but I have not forgotten what I saw in the playground this morning. Now I know how you feel about her, and why you say you hate her! I don't suppose Edie will ever forgive you, but she is a nice girl, so perhaps she may. But I cannot, and I'm sure Jesus will remember it. So you had better ask His forgiveness, too, tonight when you say your prayers. Now tell Edie you are sorry.

Both girls stood there looking like loobies, because they hadn't the faintest notion of what they were expected to do. In any case, Tod was by now just a jelly of sobs and tears.

'Say you are sorry!' hissed Miss pulling Tod towards Edie.

'I'm sorry' sobbed Tod.

'Shake hands with her, Edie, to show her that you can be a nice girl, even if your father is not a farmer.'

Edie stood and gawped. 'Shake hands, Edie!' shouted Miss. Edie burst into tears. Miss took their hands, and held them together and shook them up and down. You could have heard a pin drop in the classroom, except for Tod's sobbing and Edie's wails. But the afternoon came to an end somehow. As soon as I was let out, I rushed round to the gate of the girls' playground to wait for Tod. She and Edie came out together, both still crying, with eyes red and puffed up.

'Tod' said Edie 'Dad won't half leather me when he knows! What did we do wrong?'

Tod brushed away her tears, looking up towards the farm. 'I don't know' she said 'I reckon Miss Cornell's gone mad, or something.'

'Let's go and look at the tackle' I said, forgetting Kitch for a moment. Tod suddenly pulled herself together, as all the happenings of the day came back to her.

'No' she said, slowly – and I could see the mischief creeping back into her eyes again, red as they were with crying. 'Let's go and play on the new straw stack – and have tea in the cart-hovel. You can be mother, Edie, if you like. We can play where we like now, for ever, and ever, and ever, amen!'

And of course we could – and did.

LONG RIDES
A PENNY

I KNOW THERE'S folk who think we had nothing to do, people like us who lived in the country before everybody had a motor-car, I mean. Town folks liked to come for a holiday in the fen for a week in the summer, sometimes, but they'd soon be grumbling about all the things they didn't care for. Some of them couldn't bear the earth closets down at the bottom of the garden, and didn't go till they were forced to – and we used to laugh to hear our visitors making such a fuss if they wanted to go after it was dark, because of course there were no light anywhere. Sometimes they'd try and go down the path with a candle alight to see the way (though if Dad were about he'd usually leave a lantern ready lit against the back door). Others didn't like the shortage of water in a hot summer, at least them as were used to taps with running water. We just had tanks to catch the rainwater, and if they ran out we dipped 'frog-skin wine' from the dykes. What most people don't understand about the fen is that although there's too much water everywhere when it's wet weather, there isn't enough in a dry season. The peat turns to soft crumbly dust, and the dykes and drains dry up. In 1921, there was such a hot summer that everything dried up – dykes, drains, wells, ponds and all. We had a farm pond, but before long Dad got real worried about our animals, because all our neighbours for a very long way round had to fetch water from it for their own drinking, and of course he couldn't refuse them. When I was going down the drove one day, I saw a poor old woman on her knees down in the bottom of a dyke. She'd got her old black kettle with her, and a table-spoon, and was trying to fill the kettle for a cup of tea by letting the water seep from the mud a tablespoon at a time.

We had some visitors from a town that year – one of our cousins had got engaged and brought her young man to show him to us. We thought he was very la-di-da, and I dare say he thought we lived like animals, that particular time. You see, we'd got so short of water that summer that we could only have one enamel bowl full for washing our hands in all day, once we'd had our morning wash. So the bowl stood in the kitchen sink, and whoever wanted to wash their hands after that had to use the same water, all day. It wasn't as bad as that for long – only about a fortnight – but it just happened to be while our posh visitors were there. By the time they went back, most of them would be glad to go, and spend the last evening saying things like 'I can't think how you can abide the winter here!' or 'There's nothing going on! Every day's the same. I should go dotty if I had to live here!' – and so on.

And of course, they all thought country folk were a lot of ignorant numbskulls as didn't know a big A from a bull's foot. Well, I daresay there were a lot as hadn't got much book-learning; but even that didn't apply to everybody.

As for it being dull, we never thought so. There was always something to look forward to, right through the year. Plough-witching in January, picnics in the wood on Good Friday; the Sunday-School Anniversary, and after that the Sunday School Treat; then all the village feasts, and Ramsey Fair. When harvest was over, we started looking forward to Guy Fawkes, and Christmas only just round the corner from it, with all the family parties to go to, as well as our new toys and books.

The Chapel Sunday School treat was always held in the week after 'the Anni', in a grass field lent by one of the chapel farmers. We went to the chapel for our tea, and then after tea down to the field to play games, scramble for nuts and sweets (among the cowpats) and generally enjoy ourselves. All the grown-ups used to come as well, when they'd done work, and after the races for the children were over, they'd begin to play the old round games that had been played at such do's for

162

donkeys' years. There was 'Green Gravel' and 'There stands a lady on the Mountain', and 'There was a jolly Miller' and 'I sent a letter to my love' and 'In and out the windows' and 'Kiss-in-the-Ring'. Then perhaps somebody would bring his concertina, and the grown-ups would dance the 'Cross-hand Polka' or 'Haste-to-the-Wedding'. Our Grammam loved to dance, and the school-treat was the only chance she ever got; but Dad would take her as his partner (if he didn't happen to be supplying the music) and Tod and me would watch them springing about and keeping in step with the tune till we couldn't keep our feet still, and capered round the outside of the dancing ring, learning the steps as best we could.

Once I remember, and only once, somebody asked for 'the broomstick dance'. There were only two or three people who remembered how to do it. Grammam and another old lady tried to teach the younger ones (after somebody had fetched some brooms), but they couldn't manage the steps properly. The other old lady was Ben Munsey's mother-in-law, and when Grammam couldn't go on any longer because she was short of breath, they were going to stop; but suddenly Ben himself came through the ring of spectators, and snatched the broom out of Grammam's hands, and went to it with a will with his wife's mother. We could hardly believe our eyes, but there he was, the best dancer I'd ever seen in my life, then or now. He had never joined in anything that I could ever remember, before, but I reckon he was the same with that as he was with everything else. If he bothered to do it at all, it had got to be done properly. I'd never seen that old dance done before, and I've never seen it since, but I shall never forget Ben doing it that day. It was grand.

Now about that time, the school-treat had begun to change a bit. One or two enterprising folks in Ramsey had took to going round all the school treats, setting up stalls and selling home-made sweets and toffee, and such like. The Sunday-School teachers didn't like this at all, at first, and wouldn't let them set up their stalls; but they soon found out that all the children hung about round the stalls, outside the gate instead of joining in the games in the field, so they had to give in. Next thing was that somebody brought a set of swinging boats, and set them up as well. These people were called Hobbs, and they had a sweetstall and the swinging-boats. Mrs. Hobbs (Ol' Mis' 'Obbs) must have had a stroke or something sometime or other, because her face was twisted all round to one side, especially her mouth. She talked out of the side of it, nearly as if she was whispering into her own ear – only she didn't whisper. She shouted as loud as she could in a sort of high-pitched woman's voice like bearings as have run hot, and she never stopped from the moment they set their stall out till the last customer had spent his last penny.

'Come along now, come along boys and girls! Long rides a penny! Come along, Boys and girls, come along! Come along!'

Our Mam was a wonderful mimic, and could 'do' Ol' Mis' 'Obbs to a tee. When we got fed up playing with our things at home sometimes, we used to say 'Do Ol' Mis' 'Obbs for us, Mam', and she would. It never failed to set us all off, shrieking with laughter, even Dad (who in the ordinary way wouldn't let us laugh at anybody with anything out of the ordinary the matter with them). I don't suppose 'Ol' Mis' 'Obbs cared in the least about her face, or she wouldn't have stood there in full view at every treat and village feast for miles around. She even had her stall and swinging boats and Ramsey Fair. It was thinking about what happened at the fair, the same year as Farm Kitch got killed, thay made me remember Ol' Mis' 'Obbs and the school-treats.

The fair came to Ramsey in July, just before harvest, for three days, and nearly everybody went on the Saturday night, if they could possibly manage to save a few pennies to go with. It was another of those times when families got all together. Girls out to service took their days off so they could come home and go to the fair with their sweethearts. Married daughters from away came home with their husbands and children to be there at the fair on the Saturday night, because of course you saw all your old school friends with their families, and all the relations you didn't see anywhere else from one year's end to another. There was no way of getting to Ramsey, only to walk, and mothers set out from the bottom of the droves with swarms of children to walk across the fields. Most of the children would have a penny or two to spend, but even if they hadn't, there was plenty to see and hear, what with the stall-holders shouting, and the steam-organs grinding out their music to the flying-horses, and crowds of folk everywhere jostling and greeting each other and trying to carry on conversations at the top of their voices among the naphtha-flares, trying to be heard in spite of the music and crying babies. Most children looked forward to it for weeks, even if the long, five mile drag home afterwards by the light of a lantern made them grizzle with tiredness long before they got there.

But Tod and me had very mixed feelings about the fair. I don't know exactly how Tod felt, really, because she used to seem to enjoy it once we got there, especially if Dot was with her, or if we had a real family party, with Aunt Lizzie and Uncle Will there as well; but I hated it all. I wasn't allowed to tear about with my school mates, and Mam stopped to talk to everybody, it seemed. So I just stood about with my hands in my pockets waiting for Mam to come to the next stall. Then I had to be shown off to her friends, who all said the same silly thing. 'My! Ain't he growed, though! He does get a big boy!' or something just as silly. Tunky hated the fair from the very beginning, and used to squall or grizzle all the time Mam had got her, though she'd quieten down a bit sometimes when Dad put her on his shoulders. As soon as she was old enough, she just declared she would not go to the fair: and Mam and Dad had to arrange for her to stop with somebody as was too old to go. By the time, though, Tod and me were in our teens, and looked forward to going for quite different reasons. The year that Kitch was killed and we moved to the farm, however, the fair turned out to be an excitement of a very different kind.

Our Uncle Sam had come home, (for the first time since he'd run away when he was fourteen) with his wife, our Aunt Annie, and six children, ranging from a boy as old as me to a baby younger than Tunky. (Uncle's name wasn't Sam at all – it was Watson, after somebody Grammam had known before she married Grandad Rattles; but nobody ever called him anything but Sam or Sammy, and I don't wonder, with a name like that.) Aunt Annie fascinated us, because she was so different from most of the women we knew. She was small and fair, with a mass of curly, golden hair, and so full of life it was like watching a monkey jumping about. She spoke with a Derbyshire accent so strong that I couldn't understand her half the time and she said she couldn't understand us either, so it didn't matter. She was cheerful and merry and tough and bossy at the same time, and it was plain to us straight away that, as Mam said, she wore the trousers. Uncle Sam looked like Grandad Rattles, except he wasn't so big, and his eyes twinkled like Grammam's instead of glittering like Grandad's. He was a quiet, gentle, man and he didn't get on any better with Grandad now than he had done when he was a boy. Grandad took against Aunt Annie from the start. I reckon now that he knew he'd met his match in Aunt Annie! Grammam was in a sort of seventh heaven at having 'her boy' home again, so Grandad did everything he could possibly think of to upset her. For one thing, he wouldn't have anything at all to do with any of the children, especially the oldest boy, my cousin, except to bawl and swear at him and stop him doing whatever he happened to be doing, whether it mattered or not. As soon as I appeared, Grandad would be 'all over me', fishing in his pockets for things he'd found for me, or giving me a sixpence I didn't want and he couldn't afford. Then he'd draw me to one side and wink, and say loud enough for everybody else to hear 'An' don't you give little bloody-me-lady none of it (meaning Tod), or any o' these

166

other little bee's from Derbyshire!' Grammam used to wipe the tears away, Dad would look cross, and Mam be furious with her father – but it didn't do any good. Even I used to dislike him, at such times. But he kept out of the way a good deal while Uncle Sammy and Aunt Annie were there so Grammam was able to enjoy having her other grandchildren after all. It had been arranged that Aunt Lizzie and her husband Uncle Will should come for their holiday with us at fair-time as well so that they could see Uncle Sammy while he was at home. Grammam was going to have a real family party, for once, though she said she wouldn't go to the fair. She'd stop at home and mind Tunky and the other babies, so that their mothers could to free, and enjoy themselves.

Aunt Lizzie had come one day a couple of months earlier, about Easter time, and had brought a friend with her – a woman that was a milliner (Tod loved the new word, and told me it meant she made hats). The one she was wearing was certainly a very pretty one, and Aunt Lizzie said that Florrie was going to make her a summer one, in very light stuff, for best. So Mam said she would have one, as well. Aunt Lizzie's was going to be blue, but Mam said she would have black, trimmed with red ribbon because that was always smart. Then she asked if Florrie would make Tod a white one; and finally if Tunky could have a little one made in pink. Then they talked about Grammam, and Mam and Aunt Lizzie decided to buy her one between them, a black one like Mam's only trimmed with black flowers.

When Aunt Lizzie arrived at fair time, she bought a great hatbox with her, and out came all the hats. Aunt Lizzie looked more beautiful than ever in hers. So did Mam. Tod preened herself like a peacock, and it would have made a cat laugh to see Tunky, with her fat, solemn little face and big black eyes peering out from under her new pink chiffon hat. If you can imagine a baby owlet with its feathers all fluffed out, dressed in white satin with a pink cake on its head, that's just what Tunky looked like. Dad said if they put her in a booth at the fair and charged a penny for folks to come and look at her, they'd get enough money in an hour to pay for all the hats! Grammam was so pleased with her present that she cried and said no woman had ever had such good children as she'd got, and she wished she was going to the fair after all so that she could wear it. Mam said she wasn't going to wear hers to any fair – what if it rained? But Dad persuaded her to. I believe he didn't want Aunt Lizzie to look prettier than she did. Grammam offered to lend Aunt Annie hers to go in, but Aunt Annie said she'd rather not take the risk of getting it spoilt.

About the Thursday before Saturday fair-night, Dad, Uncle Sammy and Uncle Will all went out together somewhere, and the rest of us went round to see Grammam in her tiny little house. We could hardly all get in, and Mam and Aunt Lizzie joked about it as we went over the planks.

'I hope that old 'umbug ain't at home to spoil it all' Mam said. Aunt Lizzie didn't answer. I knew this was one thing they didn't agree on, 'cos Aunt Lizzie didn't have so many of his tricks to put up with as Mam did, and stuck up for her father if she could at all.

When we got there, he wasn't at home, as it happened but it didn't take any of us more than a minute to see that things weren't as they ought to be, and that Grammam was looking flushed and upset. She'd got a way buttoning her mouth up and pushing it forward when she was thinking hard, or 'wisening' as she called it, and in spite of her trying to be happy and cheerful, she kept doing this so often we could all tell she was in trouble of some sort.

'What's the matter, mother?' Mam asked, outright, sort of winking and nodding over towards Aunt Annie, as if to say was it Aunt Annie who was upsetting her. Aunt Annie was talking ten to the dozen to Aunt Lizzie, and there were so many of us children about that it might as well have been a Sunday school treat.

Grammam shook her head, but the big tears kept slipping

out of her eyes and going plop on to her big white apron.

'Is it Dad, again?' Mam asked, and Grammam nodded. Mam sort of growled. 'What's he been up to now?' she said. 'He's never been and gone and pawned your new hat?'

If you think this was a wild suggestion for her to make, it isn't really as silly as it sounds. A very little while before, Grandad had been in some sort of scrape again, and without telling anybody, Grammam had pawned her best frock in Peterborough, to get him out of it. Dad was so upset when he found out that he'd biked all the way to Peterborough to get it back for her. All the same, Mam's question made Grammam smile through her tears.

'No gal, no!' she said. 'My beautiful hat's safe enough!' Then she saw Tod and me standing listening and said 'Go and play with your cousins, there's good child'en. They wou'n't be here much longer.' We went a bit farther off but between us we managed to hear most of what she whispered to Mam, though when we pieced it together afterwards we couldn't make a lot of sense of it.

Aunt Lizzie and Aunt Annie sat down with Grammam and Mam in a ring, with their heads altogether in the middle. We could just catch enough snatches to be able to follow some of it.

'Who says so?'

'Mis' Taylor – Tabby Taylor. She called in to see Sammy, when she heard he were home.'

'She would!' (This was Aunt Lizzie). 'What business is it of hers?'

'She asked if I ha'n't bin well, 'cos I weren't with Jack at some flannagin's ball they'd had down at the *Golden Drop*! I said she knowed very well I never did go to public houses, and then she said as this weren't just the taproom, it were a sort o' private party, with invites, and Jack were there, havin' a real good time. An' she kep' giggling, and winking, as if she knowed something else she'd like to say, and darsn't. And then I thought on it – it were that very night as Jack never

169

come 'ome at all! Said he'd 'ad a job to do at Peterborough wi' the old pony an' cart an' got so late he'd stopped at his brother Stevie's till daylight! (She cried again.)

'Where was he then? Laying drunk on the floor o' *The Golden Drop*?' This was Mam, very indignant.

'Not 'e, my lass, not 'e! 'E'd found wairmer place atween sheets, by all accounts!' Aunt Annie's voice was grim. Grammam's tears were spilling again. Aunt Lizzie's cheeks were beginning to show a red spot, and her eyes looked like little bits of shiny black coal.

'I don't believe it!' she declared. 'At *his* age?' Grammam bridled. Aunt Lizzie had obviously said the wrong thing.

'My Jack's still a healthy an' 'andsome man!' she said. 'There's no call for you to go on like that, Lizzie. There's many a woman 'ould set her stall out for 'im, if he weren't my 'usband. Sixty's no age for a man! But he is my man – and I should never a-thought he'd a-done such a thing, never!'

'Who's the woman, then?' (Aunt Lizzie).

'Some dink-me-doll lately come from Peterborough way, called Jenet Kilby, as lives at Ramsey now. Tabby said as 'ow Jack 'ad got to know her as soon as she come, an' bin meetin' her ever since. Said the whull fen knowed on it, all except me!'

'I should like to get my tongue round Tab Taylor, upsetting poor old Mam wi' tales like that' said Aunt Lizzie. 'I'll lay there ain't a word o' truth in it! You know what Tab's like. She'd make mischief out of an ol' cat crossing the road!'

'I wouldn't put it beyond the old sod.' (This was Aunt Annie.)

'Sh! Sh! My children aren't used to such language!' (This was only true up to a point. Dad never swore, but most other men did, especially Grandad; but we were shocked, all the same, to hear a woman using such a wicked word.)

'Tabby said as 'ow Jack had arranged to meet this 'ere Jenet at the fair. Said she 'eard 'em with her own ears! I shan't be going' Grammam went on 'but you gals will. You keep your eyes open, in case you see 'im with this Jenet Kilby. But don't say a word to Sam, or Bill, or Will – 'cos I wou'n't be responsible for what any on 'em 'ould do if they was to know.'

Aunt Lizzie said she wouldn't believe a word till she had seen it with her own eyes, and even Aunt Annie said you should give even the devil his due, and everybody knowed how tales did get about so, and what about a cup of tea to cheer Grammam up?

Grammam had begun to cheer up, anyway. She said she'd forgot what a one Tab Taylor was for making mischief – though Grandad had told her a lie about where he'd been on the night o' the flannagin's ball, hadn't he? Mam said if that was all she'd got to worry about, she could rest easy, 'cos as Grammam very well knowed, he couldn't tell the truth if he tried. But that didn't mean he was after this Jenet Kilby, whoever she was. Still, it would be nice to know if there was any truth in it. Perhaps they'd find out, come Saturday fair night.

After that they got our tea, with some lovely cake called parkin that Aunt Annie had made, and Grammam was soon singing and whistling again, while Tod and Betty took turns at playing 'Can't get over the wa-l-l-l' with Aunt Lizzie.

When Tod and me got home, we tried to think what all the fuss was about, but we couldn't really make head nor tail of it. Grandad was always in the *Golden Drop* without Grammam. Women didn't usually go in pubs – Tod said they weren't allowed to. Neither of us knew Jenet Kilby, but I said she sounded like a witch. Tod said that was just what the trouble probably was. She'd witched Grandad, and got some money out of him. That's why Grammam was crying – it was nearly always money when Grammam cried. And Tod said let's leave it till after the fair, and then ask Dad about it, when Aunt Lizzie and Uncle Sammy and them had all gone home; but what with one thing and another, by the time Saturday came, we'd forgot all about Jenet Kilby.

It had been arranged that everybody should come to our house for tea, on Saturday, and then we'd all set out to walk to Ramsey together. But when Uncle Sam arrived, he'd only got his two oldest children, Tom and Betty, with him. 'Annie's decided to stop at home wi' Mother an't' littl'uns' he said. Everybody agreed that it was very kind of Aunt Annie, and very sensible, especially as she didn't know any Ramsey folks. Besides, it meant that two other children as were too young to enjoy the fair needn't be dragged all the way to Ramsey and back. So we set off in a gang soon after tea, and got to the fair about six o'clock.

It was the same as it has always been before, only worse. The men left the women and us children, almost as soon as we got there, arranging to meet them again about nine o'clock, when it would be time to go home. We had been well provided with money to spend, but neither Tod nor me wanted to spend it on the flying horses, or the swinging boats, or the penny-on-the-mat. We had to, though, because Mam kept sending us off with our cousins, who wanted to go on everything. To tell the truth, we didn't think a lot to our cousins. We didn't understand them, or their ways. They were into everything, ferreting and scratching about in places where they'd no right to be, and doing things we shouldn't have dreamt of doing. We were terrified they'd do something dreadful, and we should get the blame. So while we trailed after them, a bit miserable and sulky, Mam and Aunt Lizzie found somebody new to greet and stop and talk to, every few yards. Then they'd stand simpering about, changing the angle of their hat-pins so that everybody should notice their new hats, till it was enough to aggravate a saint. (Tod had refused to wear hers, at the last minute. She said she wanted to keep it new for next year's 'anni'.) We moved very slowly through the main part of the fair, towards the bottom end, farthest away from the gate. All the main travelling roundabouts and sideshows were at the top end, and the less exciting things were down at the bottom end where, behind the last row of stalls and things, the caravans of the fair people filled the rest of the big field.

172

We'd just about reached the bottom when we heard a familiar voice shouting 'Come along, boys and girls! Come along! Long rides a penny! Long rides a penny! Come along now! Come along! and there was Ol' Mis' 'Obbs, with her stall and swinging boats, just like at a school-treat.

Aunt Lizzie took it for granted we should want a ride and fished in her pocket for four silver threepenny-pieces she'd been saving for us. Then Mam said 'Go off by yourselves a little while, you children. You can't get lost down this end of the fair. Don't go too far away, 'cos it will soon be time to meet your dad again. Go and have a look round, and come back to Mis' 'Obb's stall by half-past-eight.' We didn't want telling twice. But Tom and Betty wanted to go on Mis' 'Obbs's swinging boats.

'Long rides a penny!' said Tod winking, and she handed her threepenny bit to Betty, looking at me in the way I knew meant she was 'up to something'. She was nodding and squinting, but I knew what she meant. She wanted me to give my threepence to Tom. Suddenly, I saw it all. If we gave them our money to go on the swinging boats, they could have six long rides apiece and we could be free of them. I never handed over my money in all my life with a better heart than when I put my tiny coin in Tom's hand. For half an hour or more, we could forget all about them.

Off they went, and while Ol' Mis' 'Obbs was obligingly getting rid of the couple who were occupying one of the boats by putting a plank under it to stop it swinging, we went round the other corner of her stall to see them safely installed before we made off without them. We stood in the shadow of the stall, with the dark field behind us where the caravans were, and the bright fair field in front. It was nearly dark now, and the lights were being put up everywhere – the naphtha flares hissing and gurgling at the back of every stall and coconut shy and rifle range and peepshow. We watched Tom and Betty being given a shove off for their first long ride, and were just preparing to set off by ourselves when

Tod grabbed my arm and pulled me back. Standing about six feet away from us was Grandad Rattles and – well, all I can say is that he was looking and acting very peculiar. He always looked crafty, and had a habit of turning his eyes from side to side – Mam used to say it was to make sure folks were watching him. He was doing that now, but in a different way. There was no doubt about it, he was *skulking*. He looked real scared, and every now and then he'd make a dive into the shadows between the stalls, or even into the field at the back, among the vans, and stand there as quiet as a mouse. Then he'd come out, and peer about into the crowd from under his cap, before suddenly turning and rushing back again into the dark where nobody could see him. Once he bolted back behind Ol' Mis' 'Obbs's stall, right by where we were standing, but he didn't see us, though we could have touched him.

'Whatever's he doing?' Tod whispered, but I couldn't answer her. We were so puzzled by him that we forgot about the fair, and everything else. It was because we couldn't take our eyes off his antics that we noticed the other fellow. Wherever Grandad was, there was this other man, within three or four yards of him. When Grandad stopped, the other one stopped, and pretended to be looking the other way. When Rattles bolted behind a stall, the other chap always moved so as not to lose sight of him – but Grandad didn't seem to know he was there. For one thing, Grandad looked straight at him several times without seeing him – you could tell that; and for another, the second chap was such a little fellow, Grandad would have made two of him in every direction. I was sure Grandad didn't even know he was there.

Tod and me slunk back to behind Mis' 'Obbs' stall so that Grandad shouldn't see us, though we wanted to see what was going to happen to him next. Tod whispered 'I reckon the little man's a pick-pocket. Let's keep watch.'

I thought about it. 'Pick-pockets would go for rich folks' I said. 'Nobody with any sense'd bother to pick Grandad's pocket.' Tod's eyes grew as big as saucers.

174

'Jed' she said 'you don't reckon Grandad's picked some-body's pocket, do you — and the other pick-pocket knows, and is trying to get whatever he's took away from him?' It seemed as if that might be the explanation. Grandad was watching for the police, and the other chap was waiting his turn to rob Grandad. It was terrible. Tod was speaking again. 'I've seen that little man somewhere before' she said 'but I can't think where.' Yes, so had I, I was sure, but that didn't help at all. We kept thinking about Grammam if the police found Grandad and took him to gaol.

Suddenly, Grandad came out from behind a stall, and bolted away from us, with the little man after him like a shadow. They'd gone out of our hearing, though not out of sight, when a strange woman, all dressed up and 'bedizened' (nearly like one of the fair women), suddenly went up to Grandad and caught hold of him. He tried to run away before she reached him, but he was too late. She hung on to him. He kept pushing her away, and it looked as if they were quarrel-ling 'cos once he sort of raised his fist to her. The other chap stood by and watched it all from a little way off, and we watched all three of them. Then Grandad broke away and came tearing towards us pushing his way through the crowd. She followed at his heels, still talking to him and looking up at him. The little man still slunk along after them. When Grandad got nearly up to us, he looked pleased and shouted out loud 'Bill! Sammy!' Then he began to run past us. We peeped out, and there on the other side of Mis' 'Obb's swing-ing boats we could see all our family party, the men as well as the women, with Tom and Betty. They were waiting for us, of course, to go home.

Grandad ran up to them as if he'd never been so pleased to see anybody in his life before. If it hadn't all been so puzzling, we should have had to laugh, because everybody, Dad in-cluded, looked so surprised. It wasn't like Grandad to go near his family, wherever they were, if he could help it, let alone make out he was pleased to see them. They sort of scattered, to take him in, and the woman stopped stunt on the edge of the group, and looked as if she didn't know what to do next. The little man went up and stood close behind her. The woman kept close to Grandad, who was pretending she hadn't got anything at all to do with him. I could see Mam and Aunt Lizzie eyeing her up and down, and showing by their faces what they thought of her hat and her feather boa and all the rest of her bedizenings, while she was looking at them, taking in their clothes (especially their hats). She sort of squared herself up, bold as brass, and reached forward, as if she was going to speak to Grandad again, or even take hold of him; but just as she moved, the little fellow bumped up against her, and she let out a shriek as you could hear right over all the other noise. It was so loud it cut right across all the other sounds – the steam organ on the roundabout, and the creaking of the swinging boats, and Ol' Mis' 'Obbs still yelling 'Come an' have a go, your mother won't know' out of the corner of her mouth, and all the crowd talking and laughing and calling to each other. She squealed out like a pig with its head in a gate, and clapped both hands to her behind and started jumping about like a parched pea in a colander. Everybody stopped and gawped and laughed, and even Tod and me came out of hiding to watch. All our family stood there with their eyes popping out like ginger-beer bottle necks, and their mouths open as if they were a parcel of real numbskulls – all except Grandad, that is. While she was still holding her bottom and shrieking, he made off one way as hard as ever the could, while the little man disappeared into the crowd in the opposite direction. Then the woman stopped yelling and dancing about. She marched straight up to Mam and said something we didn't hear. Mam looked flustered, and frightened, and all together put out.

'I never touched you!' she said.

'O yes you did!' bawled the woman. 'I never let no other woman get the better o' me yet, and I shan't let you, for all your fancy 'at!' And she suddenly made a grab at Mam's

176

beautiful new hat, to claw it off her head. The hat pin was through Mam's bun of lovely glossy black hair, but the woman tugged and tugged till the hat came off and Mam's bun was pulled all awry and draggly, with wisps hanging down.

'Here! Here! What are you up to?' Dad said, but he wasn't quick enough to save Mam from the attack. The queer woman flung Mam's hat down on the filthy ground, and then jumped on it with both feet. Aunt Lizzie rushed at her, and tried to pull her off it, but she shoved Auntie away and jumped again, and then wiped her boots on the hat, where it lay all crushed and dirty on the dusty ground. Mam had run to Dad, who was doing his best to comfort her, while Uncle Will pulled Aunt Lizzie away and Uncle Sam gathered all us children up to protect us from the mad woman, as we thought she must be. Then, all at once, she took to her heels and went off into the crowd, giving Mam's hat a last kick that sent it flying.

'Well!' Mam kept saying. 'Well!' She was trying not to cry. Aunt Lizzie picked the hat up, and tried to smooth it out. Mam took it, and put it back on her head, in a sort of daze, but her hands were trembling so much she didn't get it straight. The lovely red ribbons were all hanging down round the drooping brim, and Mam looked defeated and bedraggled like an old hen that another one has feathered.

'Whoever was she?' Mam asked, still too bewildered and frightened to be really angry, yet.

'That' said Aunt Lizzie 'that was Jenet Kilby, you may depend!'

'Who's she?' said Uncle Sammy.

'You don't have to ask *what* she is' said Aunt Lizzie. 'You can see that!'

'Come on' said Dad. 'We'd better get off home before they make the whole lot of us into a peep show.' He was right, because a lot of folks had already gathered round to stare and laugh.

As soon as we got out of the fairground, Mam began to cry about her new hat, and blamed Dad for making her wear it. He promised her that if the harvest was good he'd buy her another, an even better one. And they talked and talked about what had happened, though always in such a way as to make sure we were not to understand anything. To this day I don't know why Tod and me kept quiet about all we'd seen going on before Grandad ran up to them, or about the little man following him, but we didn't – perhaps they never stopped talking long enough for us to get a word in. It was a long and weary way home, but we got as far as Grammam's at last, where we had to go to pick up Tunky.

The moment we went in, we could see that Grammam was all right again. She was bustling about, whistling, with her eyes twinkling and sparkling. Aunt Annie was sitting in Grammam's chair, gently rocking to and fro. A big plate of rock from the fair stood on the old deal table, and Grammam was picking chips of it on her finger and sucking it between tunes.

'Where did you get your rock?' Dad asked. (He brought Grammam some toasted coconut for a fairing, because she loved sweet things.)

'Jack brought it' Grammam said. 'He's just been in and just gone out for a pint afore supper. Said as he wanted to be here when you all got back, 'cos it 'ould be so nice to have you all together for once.' She looked at Mam and Aunt Lizzie, and said. 'You were right, Lizzie. There weren't no truth in it.'

Nobody seemed to notice Mam's hat, but I knew that sooner or later somebody would start and tell Grammam the tale. Tom and Betty were put straight to bed, but Tod and me sat on the old sofa. We were so sleepy that we both drifted off into a doze. It was a burst of laughter from everybody else that roused us, and I woke in time to hear Grammam say. 'You won't forget to give me my hat-pin back again, will you, Annie? I shall prize that hat-pin for the rest o' my days!'

Tod nudged me, and we shut our eyes again, and pretended to be asleep.

'Ah' said Annie. 'It were lucky as I'd borrowed t'hat-pin. Yer see, Bill, I had to get all my hair up somehow under Sam's old cap, and it kept bundling down again do what I might. So in the end I bunched it up on top o' my head, and stuck Mother's long hat-pin right through it, sort of under the peak of the cap. Will's workaday suit fitted me a treat, and I had one o' Jack's own neck-handkerchers round my neck. I followed him from the time he got to the fair – but he spent all the time trying to keep out o' sight. I thought he were afraid of any of us seeing him, but suddenly, there she was. I knowed straight away from the looks of her that it must be this Jenet Kilby. As soon as he catched sight of her, he looked round for somewhere to bolt to, like a scared rabbit, skulking from stall to stall. It were right funny, that it were! But she see him, and come swaling up to 'im, tryin' to catch 'old of 'im an' calling 'im "Jacky-boy" and the like. He told her to bee off, he didn't want nothing to do with her, nor any of her sort. She kept telling him he'd promised to meet her at the fair, but he said that was a bee lie – she'd asked him to, he hadn't said he would. An' I don't know what would have happened if he hadn't seen you all a-standing together by the swinging boats. I were right scared then as one of you would see me and reckernise me but I did want to see what happened. I needn't have worried, 'cos nobody was takin' any notice o' me. Then I see that Jenet didn't know who any of the rest of you were, and that she was going to brazen it out with Jack in front of you, child'en and all. So I thought o' yon hat-pin, an' got behind her just in time. That'll teach her!'

Well, they laughed, and laughed, and laughed, until me and Tod started to giggle in spite of ourselves, but they didn't notice we were awake. Tod whispered 'No wonder we thought we'd seen the pickpocket somewhere before!'

'Pull yourselves together, do!' said Grammam. 'Jack'll be

back in a minute, an' I wou'n't have him know Annie had followed him for all the gold in the fen!'

'We'd better get off, I reckon, soon as he does come' Dad said. 'We've still got a mile to go, an' the child'en are wore out a'ready. So we waited to say goodnight to Grandad, who came in in a very good mood, and then set off again. Tunky, who was about three, woke up and gazed round, looking more like a baby owlet than ever. Dad set her on his shoulders, and away we all went, down the drive. It was a lovely night, soft and warm, with a great full moon following us. Nobody talked much, because everybody was too tired, I reckon, or too full of what had happened. But just before we got home, we had to cross the long narrow bendy plank over the drain. We went across it one after the other like a row of waddling ducks. When Dad was right in the middle of it, with Tunky on his shoulders, she suddenly let go of his hand and pointed with her fat little fist to the moon.

'What's the matter, my pretty?' Dad asked.

'Moon' said Tunky. 'Mammy! wouldn't the moon make us a lovely plum-pudding!'

Dad let out roar of laughter, nearly like a bull bellowing, and all the other grown-ups joined in. They just stood on that plank and laughed and I could tell then that they'd really been wanting to laugh all the way since we left Grammam's, but had been bottling it up. Then we all got to safety over the plank, and Uncle Will slapped his sides, and roared till he couldn't breathe, and Dad had to set Tunky down so he could wipe his eyes. Aunt Lizzie held her sides because they ached so, and Mam kept giving silly little lady-like giggles that made everybody else worse, partly because she looked anything but lady-like in her creased and bedraggled hat, with her hair all falling down.

'Well, as Annie says, if that hat-pin of hers don't teach Jenet Kilby a lesson, I don't know what will' said Uncle Ted: and off they went again.

There wasn't another sound in all the fen but our laughing.

I looked all round, and the fen stretched away as far as ever you could see in the moonlight, with just the dark shape of a tree or a cottage sticking up here and there against the sky. And the moon caught the water in the drain so it looked like a strip of silver ribbon, and the laughter floated out in a great wide circle as if it could go on and on till it reached the place where the starry sky rested on the black earth. I made up my mind to say to Tod in the morning that it was the best Ramsey Fair I ever remembered. I was too tired now even to laugh when Mam pulled her ruined hat down over one eye, screwed her mouth round to one side and said. 'Come along now, boys and girls, come along! Long rides a penny!' They were still laughing when at last Tod and me fell asleep, in bed.

FLITTING

IN THE LAST summer before we left the drove to go and live up at the farm on the high road, the war caught up with us. It had been going now for three years, but there hadn't been much difference in our lives because of it. In the first year, of course, we had helped to catch the German spy who was our Aunt Harriet's lodger. Dad wouldn't let us talk about that, once he'd been took away, and even that seemed as if it had all been part of a dream a long time ago. Sometimes our teacher told us about things that were happening 'at the front', and about the Battle of Jutland, but then, she told us as well about Wolfe scaling the Heights of Abraham, and King Alfred burning the cakes, and Simon de Montford riding into 'Parli'ment' on a white horse so that afterwards it was called the mother of parli'ment', and Oliver Crumwell in a black mask cutting King Charles's head off. As far as I was concerned, it all seemed a jumble of silly tales I couldn't see much sense in. Tod said that was because I didn't listen properly, and take it in. She said she liked 'hist'ry'. I used to ask her to explain it, and sometimes she could, though mostly not. I said a wolf was an animal, so how could it be a general? Tod said scornfully that this wolf was a soldier. I was still puzzled because I did know Abraham was in the Bible. We heard a lot about him in chapel. So that was scripture, not history at all. Tod declared that Miss Cornell had said this Abraham was in Canada, because that's where this soldier Wolf 'scaled' it. Mam used to scale the herrings Dad sometimes brought from Peterborough for Saturday tea. I'd watched her doing it, many a time, holding the fish by its tail and running a sharp knife backwards from its tail to its head, so that the scales all stood up and then came off on the knife, and stuck to Mam's

185

arms so that she couldn't get rid of them. What part of Abraham did this general Wolf scale? And why did it matter to us? When Tod said it was a *place*, not a man, it did make a bit more sense – after all, we lived in a place called The Heights, though it did happen to be as flat as a pancake and mostly below sea-level. Tod said I was a numbskull, and I'd better ask Dad, because he loved 'hist'ry'. So he did, and I must say he made a lot more sense of it than ever Miss Cornell could; but perhaps Tod was right, and I used to listen to him better than I did to the teacher. Usually, my head was too full of other things to bother about 'hist'ry' – like the next thing I wanted to draw and paint, or make with my meccano set or fretsaw. I wanted to know things like about how motor-cars worked, not what happened thousands of years ago. The day I saw my first aeroplane I was so excited I didn't breathe for such a long time that Mam thought I was choking, and thumped me so hard I fell over.

All the same, I did begin to understand about the war, especially when some of the young men from our fen started 'getting their papers' to go and be soldiers 'at the front'. One awful day, we heard Dad say that if they raised the call-up age much higher, he'd have to go. Mam told him not to be so silly frightening us all like that, because they wouldn't take farmers. Even he had to agree she was right, so we breathed freely again. When we had a daily paper, sometimes, Mam and Grammam would read it and cry about 'the cas'alties'; but it was really only when some of the young chaps I'd always known actually came to our house in their uniforms to say goodbye to Mam and Dad after being 'on leaf', that I suddenly realised what 'going over the top' or 'becoming a cas'alty' meant. I remember one night when three of them came together, all looking very smart with their puttees wound round their legs and their flat hats on. They told Mam and Dad a lot of funny tales that had happened to them in the trenches, but when they thought Tod and me weren't listening they told some things that weren't at all funny. They made me think about the war a lot more than Miss Cornell did.

Tunky was three, now – still as fat as butter, with a big round face with two big black sleepy-looking eyes in it. She was asleep on the couch when the three soldiers came in, and Mam left her there while she got them all a lovely meal of ham and beef and such. Then she fetched out her home-made orange wine, and they had each two or three tumblers full of it. When Mam had cleared away, they sat in a row on the edge of the sofa, leaning on the table, with Tunky still asleep behind them, and sang

'O, for the roly-poly,
Mother used to make!
Roly, poly, treacle duff,
Roly, poly, that's the stuff!
Only to think about it,
Makes my belly ache!
O, lor lummy,
I wants me mummy
The puddens she used to make!'

They stopped to have their glasses filled up with wine again, and suddenly from behind them a solemn, sleepy little voice said –

'Lor lummy! I wants my mummy' –

Tunky didn't get any further, because everybody thought it was so funny they laughed, and she stopped. But the boys wanted her to go on, though she couldn't remember any more. So they said they'd teach her another song and they stood her up on the sofa, and taught her to sing:

'Tickle me, Timothy
Tickle me, do!
Tickle me, there's a dear!
"My last train is due," said Sue

I feel like losing it, straight, I do.
I-can't-help-myself. I shall do it in half a tick;
If you don't make me laugh
I shall swallow my ticket,
So tickle me, Timothy, quick!'

Tunky learned it straight off, tune and all, only she said
'Ticker me Timoffy' and, didn't get all the words quite right
and the three all picked her up and hugged and kissed her, and
then kissed Mam and went out all in a hurry. It had seemed
such good fun when Tunky was making us laugh, but as soon
as the shed door shut behind them, Mam sat down and cried,
and Dad dropped his face into his hands like he did at chapel,
and we went all quiet, because we knew he was praying
for them. As it happened, all three of them came back after
the war, safe and sound, and that must nearly have been a
miracle.

Michaelmas Day was on October 11th, and we were going
to move from the drove to live in Grandmother's house,
come Michaelmas – at least, Dad would take over the farm
from that day, though we might not be able to move house
till Grandmother had got settled in with another one of my
aunts. It was a great adventure for us to move house, and we
could hardly think about anything else when the time got
near. But I do remember one thing that happened just before
the Great Flitting Day.

The mill that Dad ran used to be overhauled every autumn
by the firm that built it, and a man used to come from Nor-
folk to see to it. That year, when he came, I went with Dad
down to the mill, and the chap had to climb out on the sails to
mend one of the slats. I stood underneath, and looked up at
him, spreadeagled out on the top sail holding on with his legs
and feet. I wondered however he dare be there at all, so high
up, let alone leaving go with his hands to do what he had to. It
made me sweat just to see him. But when he'd finished, he
called down to Dad to let the sails turn – with him still up

there! So Dad did, and the great sails began to sweep slowly round, with the man still clinging to one of them. Then the one he was on swung right out to the side, and then came round to that it nearly swept the ground, and he was hanging head-downwards till it began to move up the other side again. He went round two or three times before Dad stopped the sails again, and he clambered down. I thought he was the bravest man I'd ever seen, and I said so to Dad. Dad said it was because his family, the Smithdales, had been building mills and working with them so long that they felt like parts of the mill themselves. They understood exactly what you could or couldn't do. He agreed that it took a lot of courage to do a thing like that, but in this man's case it was a question of skill and understanding, and it would be foolhardy for any-body else to try to copy him. Dad needn't have worried about my trying it! But Dad did go on to say that there were all sorts of ways of being brave, and it would take a lot more courage for some folks to stand up and say a few words in public than it would to go round with the mill sails. I thought about that one, and came to the conclusion, as usual, that Dad was right. There was nothing I hated more than having to 'say my piece' at 'the anni', or in a school concert, and I never talked if there were strangers about. I was terribly, terribly shy then, and have been all my life – though Tod and Tunky would both talk a donkey's hind leg off, who-ever happened to be listen-ing. In this they were like Dad, and I was like Mam, who was always shy and flustered in company, though she liked being the centre of attention all the same. I didn't!

I was not to know, though, that day down at the mill, how soon I was going to find out what it took to be brave.

The day for our flit came at last. We were all up very early in the morning, and I went with Dad up to the farm to lead back one of the empty farm carts to put the furniture in. Dad and Ben Munsey led the others, and the carts were soon standing in the yard by the side of the house waiting to be loaded. Tod had had to stop indoors with Mam, to help her carry the smaller things out, and to mind Tunky.

The men set about getting the beds to pieces and manoeuvring them down the stairs or out of the windows, while Mam and Tod bundled up the blankets and pillows and so on. Dad told us to take as many small bits of furniture as we could carry and lay them on the patch of grass behind the shed, so that he could tuck them in among the bigger stuff as they would fit in. All such stuff as glass and crockery, and other breakable things, would have to go on top of the carts. That was how it happened that the big oval mirror from over the front room fireplace came to be lying out on the grass, face up, among all sorts of other odd stuff.

Tunky was toddling about, taking it all in, as usual, with her big black eyes and a solemn, fat little face, getting in Mam's way (and everybody else's). Mam kept saying in exasperation 'Tod, will you keep that child out of my way!', and in the same breath telling Tod to go there, or bring that here, so she never did have time to see to Tunky. Every time Tunky got in Ben Munsey's way, he swore at her under his breath, and Dad pretended not to hear – while Dad himself kept saying 'Mind away, my sweetling' or 'Stan'a-one-side, my pretty', but she took no notice of anybody. She just poddled on her own way, solemn as a little owl.

Dad lifted the great hams and sides of bacon down from their hooks in the shed ceiling, and had laid them out on the grass with the mirrors and so on. This seemed to send Mam into a real 'taking', because the sunlight showed up how stained the calico hambags were.

'There's been just too much for one pair of hands to do' she kept complaining 'what with being up at the farm so much this summer, and traipsing up and down the drove all hours of the day and night! I got the new calico from Candidly Allen weeks ago to make them new hambags, but I've never had time! Whatever will folks think to see them filthy things! There's one thing, Dad – you put my sewing machine right on the top o' the last load, with the calico. I've got to get them hams fresh bagged before Harriet or your mother sees 'em, or I shall never hear the last of it. That'll be my first job, as soon as ever we have got the stuff straight ------' and so on, and so on. She kept going to the door and looking out at the hams every now and then as if she intended to sit down among all the muddle and make the new hambags there and then.

Mam and Tod had gone back upstairs to fetch some more things, and Dad and Ben were trying to fit the grandfather clock on to the top of a cart. I was holding the horse by the bridle, to make sure it didn't move just at the wrong minute, when Tunky decided to go out of the back door and inspect the hams for herself. I could see her from where I stood, poddling about and peering down at each ham in turn, with her fat little legs in black boots set wide apart for all the world as if she was judging produce in a show or something. I took my eye off her a second to see to the horse I was holding, when suddenly she let out such a scream of terror that my own skin came out in goose pimples all over just to hear it. There was no mistaking it for a cry of pain or anger – it was a shriek of fright that froze us all where we stood. Dad and Ben were on top of the cart, balancing the grandfather clock, and couldn't let go. I could see Dad was prepared to drop his end if he had to, though the clock had belonged to his great-grandfather and was one of the most precious things he owned. But I let go of the horse instead and ran. Tunky was leaning slightly forward, with her hands on her chubby knees, staring down with her black eyes so wide with fright that they seemed to take up half her face. After that first dreadful scream she hadn't moved or made another sound, though her mouth was still wide open. When I reached her, I grabbed at her, but she was quite stiff, and I realised she was holding her breath, so I hit her, hard. It seemed a year before she took her next breath, and I think I nearly died as well waiting for her, because I didn't know what else to do. I had tried once to lift her up, but she was stiff and I couldn't, till she breathed again. Then she sort of collapsed against me so I tried again. As I did so, I saw what she had seen, and nearly fainted with terror myself. She had toddled up to the big oval mirror, lying face upwards on the grass, and looked into it – and there, below her, was her own face, and beneath that a blue, bottomless pit of emptiness. My own head reeled and my stomach turned over at the awful fear of falling into this dreadful gap in the earth at my feet. My knees gave way, and Tunky and I both fell over on to the grass. Dad had reached us by this time, and tried to take Tunky out of my arms, but she wouldn't let go of me, even to go to Dad. She just clung on, so Dad helped me up, and somehow or other, we got indoors – though of course there was nothing left to sit on, even there. Tunky was crying now, but I felt better as soon as I'd got solid ground beneath me and solid walls, that kept still, all round me. I told Dad what had frightened us, and he went out to take a look himself. Even he didn't feel too good, looking down into that mirror – and if you don't believe me, try it for yourself some time! (Tunky never forgot that experience. She says now that she learned the meaning of infinity and eternity in that split second. She has had a phobia about heights ever since, and couldn't be persuaded to fly 'with that blue emptiness all round her' if she could have a fortune at the end of the trip.)

Dad went back to his loading, but Tunky wouldn't let go of me, so I took her into the garden, and sat her on the lowest bough of the old apple tree, with her arms round my neck, and she soon cheered up. It seems now as if the whole of that day is like a picture that I can still look at, because if I shut my eyes I can be back there in the garden under the apple tree with Tunky, and see and hear everything going on round us as clear as I could then. I remember (and so does Tunky) that I sang 'If you were the only girl in the world' to her, and she joined in, where she could. (All three of us must have had a pretty good ear for a tune, I think.)

Mam and Tod went up the drove with the first cartloads, to be at the other end to tell the men where to put things, but Tunky would not leave me. (I think she must have thought

I'd saved her life!) Of course Dad wanted me to lead one of the carts, but he wasn't going to upset Tunky again, so Tod had to do it, and I had to mind Tunky till the empty cart came back, which I was not too pleased about. However, everything from the house was packed at last, and we were ready to set off. At the very last minute, Dad remembered 'Home Kitch' and her brood of kittens, about six weeks old, that were in the little barn. He couldn't find anything to put them in, but he solved the problem. The tail-board of the cart had been let down, and he cleared a little space among the hams and sides of bacon that were piled on it. Then he lifted Tunky into the space, so that her chubby little legs in their black boots hung down over the tail-board, and he showed her how to gather her skirt up all round her to make a little nest. He plonked Kitch and her three kittens into Tunky's lap, and stroked and fussed the old cat till it seemed she understood what was happening, and settled down to suckle her babies. I had to walk behind the cart, keeping hold of the tail-board, to see that neither Tunky nor the cats fell off; and away we went, with the cart rocking from side to side as its wheels fell into the ruts of the drove. After a mile or so of this, we reached our new home at the farm.

The rest of the day doesn't matter to the tale, except to say that by the time it began to get dark, we had moved in. Of course, we had been living up there during the day for most of the summer, so it didn't really seem all that strange, except that it was our own furniture there now, and not Grandmother's. Mam's hams lay on the pantry shelves, still in their old bags, and as soon as ever we'd had our supper, she asked Dad to put her sewing machine on the table, because she was going to make new hambags.

'What, tonight?' Dad asked, as if he couldn't believe it. Mam nodded. 'You know as well as I do that Harriet'll be up here first thing in the morning to see what's going on' she said. 'And I'm not having her telling everybody in the fen about them mucky hambags. It won't take me long!' So he didn't argue any more. Tunky had fallen asleep in Mam's big chair, so Mam didn't rouse her to put her to bed, in case she wouldn't settle in the strange room. Tod had gone into the front room, and was playing hymns on her precious piano, with its candles alight in their special candlesticks, as if she couldn't wait to try the piano out in its new situation. The sound came very faintly through to the rest of us in the house-place for a little while, and then stopped. Perhaps Tod was asleep on the piano stool.

Dad was sprawled out in his chair, with his legs straight in front of him, and was soon as fast asleep as Tunky. No wonder – he'd been up at four that morning, to go up to the farm and help with the yardwork. Then he'd been lifting furniture about all day long, and walking up and down the drove, till it was time to do the yardwork and milking again in the evening. We'd had a bite of supper, and he'd had a wash, so it would have been quite nine o'clock in the evening before he sat down at last for a rest, and Mam started making her new hambags. I sat at the table, the other side from Mam and her machine, with a big bound copy of *The Boys' Own Paper* in front of me, copying a picture from it. I was facing the big window that looked out on to the doorway and down the garden, and beyond that to the fields that were now ours. We hadn't got the curtains up yet, because Dad hadn't been able to fix the big mahogany curtain pole, and from where I sat, I could see the reflection of everything inside the room in the dark glass – the oil lamp on the table with its bowl of orange light, Mam's back as she turned her sewing machine handle and the big blue chair with Tunky asleep in it in the corner. Outside, it was already dark, though there was a full moon rising in a soft, dark blue autumn night sky.

The machine whirred away, and Dad snored. When Mam had finished the first bag, she laid it aside, and picked up the length of new unbleached calico. She took her scissors and made a little nick in the selvedge, and then took the calico in both hands and tore it apart. It ripped with a loud, rough, tearing sound, and Dad opened his eyes and looked around him in a puzzled dazed sort of way till he'd remembered where he was; then he sank back and went off again. Nobody spoke, and my eyes began to droop, too, so that I dozed off with my head on my book and my arms on the table. Every time Mam ripped her calico we all roused and wished she wouldn't do it, but we all knew it was no good trying to stop her.

Then there was the ripping noise again – only ten times louder, and ten times longer than it had been before. I woke, and Dad sat bolt upright in his chair, and said 'Lawks, Mam! *Need* you make such a row?' Mam was opening her mouth to say it wasn't her, when it happened. The window in front of me shook, and a great 'blash' or orange light lit up the trees in the garden, and then the whole fen for as far as I could see. A huge ball of flame was rising from one of our farm fields – the one just the other side of our only grass field, which lay directly behind the house.

'It's a BOMB!' Dad said, and clawing out of his chair, he rushed outside. Tod appeared from nowhere, Mam grabbed Tunky who had already woken up – and we all followed Dad on to the doorway, and from there down the path to the gate that led to the fields. The bomb was still burning, throwing its awful yellow, flaring glare for miles, it seemed, over the flat land, and up into the sky – and there, moving slowly and sedately across the deep, moonlit blue was the long, dark shape of a Zeppelin. It was so low you felt you could have hit it with a stone. We could see it as plain as if it had been broad daylight.

We all clung to Dad, gibbering with fright – but he scrambled free and pushed us away from him, leaving us standing there. He knew that the animals in the yard would be panicking with terror and might kick and injure each other, or leap the fence and get lost, or fall in a dyke.

'Bill. Don't leave us!' Mam said, but he called back as he ran.

'It's only a h'incendiary! The Zepp's gone over now! It can't turn quick enough to drop another here! Go back into the house!'

We didn't. We just stood there, huddled round Mam, and watched the Zeppelin sailing across the sky. The bomb, about a quarter of a mile away, was still burning, though not so fiercely as at first; but by its glow I could see all our faces, white and scared, with Tunky clinging round Mam's neck and Tod and me as close to her as we could get. She suddenly seemed to realise that the bomb was showing us up – of course, we all believed that the Zeppelin had come all the way from Germany just to get us. (Tod and I both had the same thought, as we checked afterwards. We thought straight away that it was somebody trying to get revenge on us for our part in helping to trap the spy.) So Mam began to scurry back inside the gate, under the trees where the Germans couldn't see us.

'*Come on*, Jed!' she said, when I didn't move to follow her.

'I can't, Mam' I said. 'My legs won't work! My knees are knocking together!' They were, too. For the second time in twelve hours I'd found out where being frightened to death took hold of me. I should certainly not have been any good clinging to a turning mill-sail with my legs and feet!

When we did get back to the house, we could hear voices out on the road, and went to look. All our neighbours had bundled out of bed, and were standing about in groups on the road, all talking about 'the Zepp' and 'the bumb' (of course, in our fen, a bomb would be called a 'bumb', just like a pig (hog) would be 'an ol' 'ug', and people called Onyett always referred to as 'Ungett': 'over' was pronounced 'uvver' and so on).

When Dad had made sure everything was safe in the yard, he joined us on the road. The other men all clustered round him, to ask him what he thought about it all. He was making up his mind what to say when the ground seemed to shake beneath our feet, and the sound of two heavy explosions, muffled by distance, but none the less real, reached our ears. Well, folk scattered like a lot of old hens when a fox is after them. Women squeaked and flapped about, running, like women usually do, sort of straight-legged and awkward, in all directions. The men skulked with their heads down in their shoulders, and ran into the shadow of a barn like mice making for their holes. One woman that had a bad hip and dropped down on one leg when she walked (we always called her 'Mis' 'Oppity-kilt') ran up the road nearly as far as the school before she found out nobody else was with her, and turned round and came back, dot-and-carry-one in the moonlight, as if Old Nick his very self was after her.

'That lot were explosives', Dad said. 'I wonder where they dropped them!' I could hear that he was worried.

'What the 'nation dew they want to drop bumbs about here, for?' one of the men asked.

'D'yer reckon they'll come uvver 'ere agin, Bill? Come back agin, I mean?' It was what we all wanted to know.

'Well' said Dad. 'I sh'd think they must have got rid of all they were carrying, now. They'll be headin' for home.'

'We might as well go back to bed, then,' somebody said, and Dad agreed. So we trooped back into the house, but Dad said nothing about anybody going to bed, though by this time it was nearly midnight. We had a cup of tea, and messed about in a sort of uneasy way, tired as we all were. It was plain to me that Dad wasn't prepared to go to bed, and Mam darn't go without him. In the end, she asked him, and he said he reckoned the Germans had been looking for the new aerodrome, that was only just behind our farm, and had dropped the incendiary to show them if they were near. They had been – very near, but not quite near enough. They'd overshot it by about a mile; but he was worried that there might be more than one Zepp looking for it, so he would stop up just in case we got the real bumbs next time. Mam lay down on the sofa, and cuddled Tunky to sleep again. Tod curled up in Mam's chair, and I stretched out on the old pegged hearthrug with

Home Kitch and her kittens. We were all dead beat, and it was daylight when we woke, though Dad had been up for hours.

As soon as he'd sluiced his face and made us a fire, Dad went down to the field where our bomb had fallen. (There were very few bombs dropped on England, apart from a few in London, in the Great War. We were very proud, afterwards, that we'd had one dropped on us.) He came back soon, carrying 'the bumb'. It was all black with soot and grime, where it had burnt itself out. It was a cylinder, about eighteen inches high and seven or eight inches across, like an oversized cocoa-tin with wire-netting round it, and a sort of wire handle over the top. Dad brought it up to the house to show us, and then took it round the stood it in the cart-hovel. Then he got on with his yardwork.

When the postman came walking up the road from Ramsey, he brought more news with him (as he usually did). The Zepp had dropped its load of 'hexplosives' about five miles away, as the crow flies. A train had been travelling down the main line towards London, and the fireman had opened his firebox, (so 'they' said – though how they found out is still a mystery) to coal up. The Zepp's crew had seen it, and tried to bomb the line, as they had missed the aerodrome that was their real target. They hadn't hit the line either. Their bombs landed in a farmyard, and killed five pigs. Now this did seem to put the fat in the fire. The fen was in a ferment of indignation, to think the 'bee-ing Germans' should come and take a man's living away, like that! Pigs as 'ad been brought up by hand, very likely, said the women, and were intended for next winter's pork pot! Lloyd George really should do something about it. Suppose it had been the farmer's hosses, instead of his pigs? He'd have been ruined! (Dad and his friends didn't know whether to be aggravated at such simple-minded views, or to laugh. I reckon they must have decided to laugh, because afterwards (especially when talking about the prisoners-of-war that were beginning to come into our district) one or the other would put on Mis'

Oppity-kilt's voice and say 'Ah! Remember as they killed them five pigs!')

As soon as the postman had left us and gone on his long walk all round the fen, the police from Ramsey arrived, and demanded to be taken to the place where the bomb had fallen. Dad said he would take them, of course, but the bomb itself was now in the cart-hovel, because he'd fetched it up.

Well, you never did hear such a to-do! The policeman reprimanded Dad very severely, for meddling with things he didn't understand, and 'destroying valuable evidence'. Dad kept taking his cap off, and ruffling his hair, and putting it back on, explaining that he knew as it was only 'a hincendiary bumb', and that it had been burnt out hours and hours before he'd touched it, and anyway there it still was for them to look at now if they wanted to, in the cart-hovel. People were already beginning to come from all over the fen to look at it. The police cleared them all out of the yard, and made them stand on the road. They ordered Tod and me (and Mam and Tunky) back into the house, and tried to send Dad away as well, though he wouldn't go. Then they fetched the bomb out (with a great show of caution), and placed it in the open space between the pig-place and the corn stacks and the pond. After that they fixed up a pump, and began to pump water on the bomb from the pond. It was a big pond, but they very nearly emptied it, before they were satisfied. The pond was empty and the yard was flooded, even all round the bottoms of the precious corn stacks, but nothing Dad could say or do would stop them. I don't know that I ever saw Dad more exasperated and helpless than he was with those police officers that day! We had watched it all happening from the landing window, that looked out over the yard. The road outside the yard was getting thick with people arriving 'to see the bumb', and Mam suddenly had an idea. She organised Tod and me to help, and to it we went.

Mam's sewing machine still stood on the table, where it had been when 'the bumb' fell. Tod was sent to look for an old pillow-slip, one of Dad's Sunday handkerchiefs, and a bit of red hair ribbon. I was told to find an empty cocoa-tin, and stick a bit of my precious drawing-paper all round it. Mam sat down to the machine, and in no time we had Tunky fitted out as a Red-Cross nurse, with a little white apron made out of the pillowslip with a red ribbon cross on it, and Dad's handkerchief also with a cross, pinned round her head. I painted a big red cross on the cocoa-tin, and made a notice that read:

PeNNy TO See THe BoMb.

Then I made a slit in the lid of the tin, and put the first penny in.

As soon as the police were satisfied they'd really put the bomb out, they left Dad to clear up the mess, and away they went. Then before Dad could open the gate to let the crowds in, Mam carried Tunky out and set her right in the middle of the gateway, shaking her tin and saying solemnly 'Penny for the bomb! Penny for the Red Cross!'

She was very good, and took the folks's fancy. They put so many pennies in her tin that it had to be emptied two or three times because it was too heavy for her to shake. Dad was real pleased at Mam having such a clever idea, and acting on it so quick. Not that he need have worried about catching the early birds because more and more people arrived, in carts and buggies, traps and even one or two motor cars, as the day wore on.

Now the stack yard blocked the view of the field in which the bomb had fallen, and the gate between the stackyard and the grassfield was also out of sight behind the stacks. When it was nearly dockey time, and people were still arriving, Dad had another idea. He sent me into the house for another tin and to make two more notices quick. One said simply:

GeNTleMen ONly

and had an arrow directing them down to the gate out of sight behind the stacks. This notice we pinned up on the cart-hovel. Of course, all the women read it, and pretended they hadn't seen it, and took no notice when their men kept disappearing. But round by the gate there, I stood with my Red Cross tin, and on the gate was another notice, which read:

YOu HaVe PAiD A PeNNy To
See THe KAiSeR's BuMb.
NoW Pay AnoTHer TO See His BuMb-HoLe.

Well, that tickled the fancy of the men, I can tell you, and whether or not they went down to look where the bomb had fell, they all put a penny in my tin, just for the joke. At the end of the day, I'd took nearly as much for the Red Cross as Tunky had.

We might be fen tigers and clodhoppers, but in our own way we'd thumbed our noses at Kaiser Bill good and proper, and everybody felt better for it. There's no doubt about it, our Dad was 'a cure, an' no mistake', as most people said. Folks have never forgot the things he used to say and do. None of our family ever forgot the day we flitted, either – and no wonder!

THE SILVER
NEW NOTHING
AGAIN

SO MANY THINGS happened the year that we moved from down the drove that I've got them a bit out of turn. It was one hot Saturday afternoon, soon after we moved, that Old Oamy turned up again.

Dad had been at work from early morning till late at night all the week, and he had gone nearly the colour of a Red Indian with the sun. The men knocked off work a bit earlier, if the weather promised fair, on Saturdays. Then Dad came home and had a bath, and after tea we sat out on the brick doorway in the golden evening light.

Dad was sitting out there by himself while Tod and me were being bathed before Sunday. We were just about ready to join him on the doorway, when we heard the musical boom of Old Oamy's voice. We rushed to the door just in time to see Dad reach out and catch the old man by both arms to stop him from falling.

'Get a chair, quick, Jed' he said, and as soon as I took it near, Dad lowered him on to it. He thanked Dad as courteously as ever, and said 'A giddy turn. I've had several of them just lately.'

'You ain't well, I can see' said Dad, looking very worried. 'I reckon as I'd better put the pony in the trap and get you to a doctor straight away so that they can get you to the infirmary before it's too late.'

Oamy laid his hand with its long fingers on Dad's brawny sunburnt arm.

'It's too late already, my friend' he murmured. 'And *you* wouldn't send me to the infirmary to die, would you? That's why I came this way again. I trusted you to understand. I've lived more than half my life now under the open sky by day and under the stars at night. Don't condemn me to death inside four walls.'

Dad said no more, but when Mam saw Oamy close to, she took the sandwiches she had cut back again into the kitchen and set about getting him some hot milk with brandy in it. Tod and I could see for ourselves that he was ill, and we didn't expect him to tell us any tales, but we'd never been anywhere close to a person that was likely to die before, and we couldn't help being curious. Then the milk and brandy seemed to revive him a lot, and he soon began to look quite like himself again. Without being asked, he began to undo his bundle. He left the rest of its contents lying on the ground at his feet, but he picked up the little box and sat with it in his hands, running his fingers round it and stroking it as he sat in the mellow evening sunshine.

It was as if Tod simply couldn't help herself. She leaned forward and touched Oamy, and said 'What's in your little box?'

'Sh! Sh!' said Mam and Dad and me, all together, because we didn't want her to worry the poor old fellow at all.

He looked down at her, a bit sadly I thought, but he smiled at her like he nearly always did when she spoke to him.

'I've told you many a time before, my pretty' he replied. 'It's a silver new nothing to wear on your sleeve.'

'Oh,' said Tod, nearly crying, I could tell. 'Oh! I thought you'd tell me the truth, the real truth, tonight. Everything's different now, and I thought you'd answer different, too. Why doesn't anybody tell us the truth?' She began to get up, trying not to cry.

The tramp put out a long arm, and held her where she was. They looked at each other as if each of them was seeing somebody they'd never really noticed before. When Tod sat down again she sat so close to him that her head was almost resting on his knee, and he brushed her hair back out of her eyes before he spoke.

'It is the truth, my pretty one' he said. 'What the box con-

206

tains is nothing of any value to anybody in the world but me.'

Mam had fetched herself a chair and sat where she could see the tramp and Tod both at once. I don't think she liked Tod sitting so close to him, but even she could feel the strangeness that had come over both of them. I still sat on the doorstep where I always did, and Dad dropped down on one knee and rested with his chin in his right hand and his right elbow in his left hand, which rested on the other knee. This is how he always took a breather in the fields, and he could stop like it, without moving, for hours if he wanted to, like when he was sitting up with a sick animal at night. And the golden evening sun shone down round us all, as if we were trapped in a picture, with time standing still forever. Perhaps it did for a little while, that evening.

The tramp's old white head fell suddenly forward, and the hand that held the box grew limp, and let it fall. Tod picked it up.

'He's gone to sleep,' she said to Dad. 'Shall I wake him up?'

'No,' said Dad. 'Let him alone. The poor old fellow's ill – and he knows it. But he knows what he's doing, and I sha'n't interfere. Put the box back on his knee, so that he can feel it the minute he wakes.'

'I hope he does wake up,' I said.

'So do I' said Tod. 'I want to see inside the box.'

We waited, a very long time, it seemed to me. The sun was getting low now and had lost some of its warmth. Dad got up, moving as quietly as a cat, and fetched from an outhouse a couple of old blankets he kept there to use on nights when he had to sit up with a calving cow or a farrowing pig. He wrapped them gently round the thin old body of the tramp and dropped again to his resting position on one knee. Mam sat more still and quiet than I ever remember her doing before or since, because she was a busy sort of person, and not much of a one for sitting still in the ordinary way. It was as if Old Oamy had cast a spell on us all and we couldn't break it until he let us go.

After about a quarter of an hour, which seemed like eternity to Tod and me, he roused again. His hand searched immediately for the box, and as soon as he had found it he smiled down at Tod and then looked round at Dad.

'That was a kind thought, my friend,' he said, indicating the blankets, 'and I thank you, if thanks from such as I am now are of any value to anybody.'

'Show us what's in the box' said Tod, urgently.

'Let him have another hot drink first' said Mam, and again she fetched him more milk with brandy in it. I could smell it, and when he tasted it he gave her such a sweet, grateful smile that we all felt paid for something we hadn't done.

Oamy's old hands fumbled with the little box, and suddenly there it was, open in front of us. I reckon Tod's gasp was only one of disappointment, but she had a lot of sense, and never let on what she'd expected to see. All that lay in the box was a tiny scrap of blue silk with a few silver threads hanging from it.

It was Dad who asked what it was, and why it was so precious.

'It's just a family treasure' he said. 'A remembrance of what once was, and never again can be. There was a time when my family ranked high in the land, with a proud name and our own armorial bearings. Our coat of arms was worked in silver on a blue silk armband that one of my ancestors wore at a battle, five hundred years and more ago. That's all that's left of it, but you can make out a bit of the motto still, here and there.'

The long speech had exhausted him, and he fell silent, staring, as we all were, at the pathetic shreds in the box.

When he looked up again, it was me who said, unbelievingly 'Do you mean that's five hundred years old?'

He nodded. Tod leaned forward and touched the silk strands, looking at him for permission as she did so. He smiled – it seemed with pleasure, and he let the box lie open on his knee. But Tod had picked up the bit about the motto. Anything in words had a fascination for her.

'What was the motto?' she asked. 'What did it say?'

He drew himself up, till he sat straightbacked in the old chair. Draped with our old blankets he might be, but he looked like one of King Arthur's knights holding a golden goblet at the Round Table.

'Ce que je peux faire, ça ca je dois' he said. We looked at each other, uncomprehending, thinking he was off his head and rambling in his mind. He caught the look.

'It is in French' he said.

Tod was enthralled. 'Say it again' she whispered. He rested his back against the chair, and looked down at Tod, repeating slowly 'Ce que je peux faire, ça ca je dois'.

'What does it mean?' she said, and then said it herself. She'd learned it, just like that. It seems to me now that nothing could have pleased the old man more than to hear her say it.

'What does it mean? Let me see. I suppose the nearest I can get to it in English would be "What I can do, that I must do".'

He shut the box, and secured the little silver clasp.

'So now you know' he said. 'I owed it to you to explain. You have treated me for many years now as if I was still the gentleman that I was born, not the ragged wanderer of the roads that I am. But then, what is a gentleman, when all is said and done?'

He looked at us all in turn, and last of all at Dad – a long, long look that Dad returned. Tod said afterwards it reminded her of a picture she'd seen somewhere of The Black Prince knighting somebody on the field of battle.

Then Oamy struggled to his feet, and Dad got up to steady him.

'Thank you again, my friend' Oamy said. 'I'm ready for the barn, now. I need a long, deep sleep.'

Dad picked up the blankets and the bundle. 'I sha'n't lock the doors tonight' he said.

'No need,' the old man said, and his blue eyes twinkled. 'I

promise you'll find me still there in the morning – on my word as a gentleman.'

And of course Dad did. He found the barn doors wide open and the old man sitting facing them where he could see the stars to the last, with the box clasped in his hand.

Dad had closed the barn doors, then, and come in to tell that he was off to Ramsey on his bike to inform the police.

I wanted to cry, but I didn't because somehow it seemed that Oamy wouldn't have liked that. Tod didn't either, though her lip quivered and she couldn't speak.

It was Mam who cried, with tears splashing down on to her apron front. She looked accusingly at Dad.

'You should have gone for the doctor last night' she said. 'You could see how bad he was!'

Dad nodded. 'Ah, that's what he trusted me for. I reckon he knowed that any real genuine old fen tiger would understand that it meant to him to be proud, and free, and independent. It were little enough to ask, when all's said and done, and I wasn't going to let the poor old fellow down at the end. What I can do, that I must, like him. So there you are!'